THE **ASSASSIN**

THE **ASSASSIN**

....

A STORY OF RACE AND RAGE IN THE LAND

OF APARTHEID   HENK VAN WOERDEN

....

Translated by Dan Jacobson

METROPOLITAN BOOKS

Henry Holt and Company

New York

Metropolitan Books
Henry Holt and Company, LLC.
Publishers since 1866
115 West 18th Street
New York, New York 10011

Originally published in Holland in 1998 by Uitgeverij Podium, under the title
Een mond vol glas.

Library of Congress Cataloging-in-Publication Data

Woerden, Henk van, 1947–
　　[Mond vol glas. English]
　　The assassin : a story of race and rage in the land of apartheid / Henk van Woerden;
translated by Dan Jacobson.—1st American ed.
　　　p.　　cm.
　　ISBN 0-8050-6631-4 (hc.)
　　　1. Tsafendas, Demitrios, 1918–1999. 2. Assassins—South Africa—Biography.
　3. Verwoerd, Hendrik Frensch, 1901–1966—Assassination. 4. South Africa—Politics and
government—1961–1978. 5. Apartheid—South Africa.　I. Jacobson, Dan.　II. Title.
DT1949.T78 W6413 2001
839.3'1364—dc21   00-069534

Henry Holt books are available for special promotions and premiums. For details
contact: Director, Special Markets.

Designed by Fritz Metsch
Frontispiece photograph of Demitrios Tsafendas, circa 1922, by Liza Key

First American Edition 2001

Printed in the United States of America

10　9　8　7　6　5　4　3　2　1

CONTENTS

THE **ASSASSIN**

1   THE EMIGRANTS

On 11 February 1955 a man could be seen wandering about the streets of Hamburg, Germany. Sometimes he halted and stared up at the branches of trees. He wore a hat but no overcoat. Absorbed in conversation with himself, he crossed Langenhorner Chaussee. It was shortly after nine in the evening; the street was empty and ill-lit. A half hour later he entered the main gate of General Hospital and made his way to the emergency ward.

In broken German, speaking excitedly, he told his story to the receptionist. He had swallowed twenty sleeping pills, he said. Exactly twenty.

Damp snowflakes clung to his frizzy hair.

Dr. Hans Nachtwey, the doctor on duty, thought the man must be either a Turk or a Syrian. He was big, with a swarthy complexion, a large nose, and a double chin. His jacket was buttoned tightly across his stomach. He swayed back and forth on his chair, his arms clamped around himself. Nachtwey examined his reflexes and the pupils of his eyes. The contents of his stomach would have to be pumped.

His father was African, his mother Greek. Or so the doctor understood him to say. This was noted down. Later in the evening Dr. Nachtwey recorded some other particulars about the patient. He carried a passport in the name of Demitrios Tsafendon. He was born in Lourenço Marques, the capital of Portuguese East Africa, in 1918.

The man's agitation did not leave him. Sitting in his chair, he wept, clapped his hands to his ears, arched his back, and uttered incomprehensible cries. Occasionally, without seeming to gain any relief, he drew deep breaths into his chest. During calmer spells he let his body slump forward, as if his head had grown too heavy to hold upright. One of his hands remained on his stomach, forgotten; the other, thumb trapped inside his clenched fist, rested on the arm of the chair.

"Do you know anyone in the city?" Dr. Nachtwey asked.

"I've got no problems," the man answered hesitantly, in English.

Everything he said came out in fits and starts. What he would like to do, he claimed, was to go back to southern Africa. But it was too late now. Couldn't the doctor see how sick he was?

He opened his eyes wide: watery, amber-colored eyes.

"It's been like this since 1937. I can't help myself. I can't defend myself. I'm always tired, always exhausted. It's eating away at me. Can't you see? And no one believes what I say. I used to have muscles; now all I've got is flab. I'm not a man anymore, just half a man."

Suddenly he burst into a screech, followed by convulsive

pants and moans. There was a snake in his stomach. For years he'd carried a worm or demon inside him. Yes, he'd been examined by the doctors, many times. But they'd found nothing. It had hidden itself too deep inside him. In the early morning he could hear it talking to him. Sometimes during the day too. He could feel it struggling in his guts.

"I'm just half a man," he said again. "I'll never recover now."

"The patient is thirty-seven years old and appears to be in good physical condition," the doctor wrote. And beneath that, in an almost illegible hand: "Delusional psychosis."

"Delusional. Deeply confused." The initial diagnosis was left unchanged. Tsafendon—or Tsafendas, as he also called himself—was placed in the closed wing of the hospital. Inquiries made at the Hamburg Hospital for Tropical Diseases revealed that he had been examined for a tapeworm a year previously, after making similar complains about his stomach. That examination had shown the parasite tormenting him to be wholly imaginary.

The man did not smoke or drink; physically his constitution was sound. Medicated with opiates and tranquilizers, he nevertheless walked in his sleep. Sometimes, standing upright, he sank into trances so deep he would lose control of his bladder and bowels; he would appear not even to notice what had happened.

At the end of the month the medication was discontinued, though no improvement in his condition had been discerned. The patient refused to get out of bed and was always ill-tempered. He barely ate. Those who tried to talk to him sooner or later heard the story of the tapeworm. Nothing would rid him of it. There were also these little hairy worms, he told a nurse, that wriggled across his field of vision. They were like curly lines that would not disappear. Why did they never leave him alone? As for the dragon in his stomach— that had crawled into him many years before. Since then he had been its prisoner. It had taken possession of him.

"I've even drunk poison to get rid of it," he said in confidential tones. "Two meters of tape came out, into my underpants. But the head still remained inside. Look, they operated on me for it." And he lifted up his pajama top to show the scar of an appendix operation.

After another two weeks his condition appeared to deteriorate further. "He urinated in the hall. He does not talk. He does not eat." Several times the attendants had to restrain him physically. Finally it was decided to administer electroshock treatment.

Spring came. Hamburg thawed. With the change of season Tsafendas became calmer. Slowly the storms in his head died down. He slept regularly and suddenly began to eat enough for two. His melancholy changed to a sort of nervous alertness. Even the imaginary beast in his belly retreated into the background of his consciousness. He was able to laugh, at times, with some of the hospital staff about his stupid fantasies. He winked at the nurses. He had an attractive glance under dark, caterpillar-like brows. When he felt like it he would tell stories, sailors' yarns, about his experiences. Stories of wild journeys, of Alexandria, Lourenço Marques, many crossings of the Atlantic and Indian Oceans. And about the Cape of Good Hope, "Cabo da Bona Esperança," as he called it, with an unusual, hissing emphasis. He would sing little songs the listeners could not understand but found charming nevertheless. They liked to hear him sing. They did not know what language he was singing in.

One morning he stood by the window, looking out. He held his head a little to the left, like a solemn ibis keeping watch over the gardens of the institution. When one of the nurses found him and asked him to come to the table for breakfast, he continued to stand there. In his best German, he asked her to pardon him for his sickness. She responded with a reassuring pat on his plump shoulder.

Halfway through May he was moved to another part of the Ochsenzoll clinic, the hospital's psychiatric center, where, in expectation of their discharge, patients were watched less closely. He offered to carry out small tasks for the staff. And he was allowed to go for walks through the park and the woods nearby. Now that the fever had died down, the nurses saw him as an affable fellow, a poor seaman who had touched bottom.

On the morning of 6 June 1955, Tsafendas bade a polite farewell to them. He was healed, out in the streets once more. The chestnut trees on both sides of the Langenhorner Chaussee had already shed their flowers. He wore a faded cinnamon-colored suit. A taxi took him to the center of town.

More than eleven years later, in Cape Town, in the chamber of the South African House of Assembly, Tsafendas would kill Dr. Hendrik Verwoerd, the country's prime minister, with four wild stabs of the knife in his right hand.

....

The sixth of September 1966 is inscribed sharply in my memory. At a few minutes before three in the afternoon the regular programs of the South Africa Broadcasting Corporation were interrupted by an urgent news item. The prime minister had been attacked during a parliamentary session. It was not yet known whether or not Verwoerd had survived.

I wandered through the botanical gardens toward the center of the city. Outside the parliament building, at the end of a long, shady avenue, there was no sign of anything unusual. The spring sunshine fell indifferently on the neoclassical pediment of the building. Squirrels skipped along the gutters. I went on farther, heading for a bookshop on Long Street. Here and there groups of people stood around radios. They spoke in low tones. An hour went by. Another thirty minutes. The stillness of the town was palpable. It is true: an entire country can hold its breath. Public life had come to a halt. An unfocused anxiety seemed to rustle through the streets.

Shortly after four o'clock it was announced that the father of the nation had passed away. The architect of apartheid was dead. The Verwoerd era was over. No one dared rejoice openly. However, many did so secretly.

In the evening I went to a small party in the upper town, above District Six, Cape Town's vibrant colored area, where racial mixing persisted in defiance of the rigid apartheid strictures. The mood in the room was one of great elation. It did not occur to anyone to doubt that the murder was the expression of deep dissatisfaction with everything the Afrikaners and their Nationalist Party stood for. Dissatisfaction—hatred, rather—was easy to feel. It went with being a student in those days. Someone upstairs was keeping watch on the street below. Around the corner a black Austin had been seen with the silhouettes of two security policemen in it. A girl who had previously seemed perfectly sensible to me began to outline a plan of action for us in case the police burst into the house. Her voice was breaking with excitement. Her boyfriend of the moment, the journalist Gordon Winter, egged her on. (Later, much later, we were to learn that he was a police informer; eventually he chose to "confess" all in his book *Inside BOSS: South Africa's Secret Police.*)

I retreated to the little kitchen. The hectic tone of the company roused in me a kind of loathing. Perhaps it was the lighthearted glee with which they were speaking of their plans that got me down. Perhaps jealousy also had something to do with how I felt. These students came from a comfortable, English-speaking background. They knew nothing of how life was really lived in the impoverished, racially mixed suburbs in which I had grown up—on the wrong side of the tracks, as people said. They had never set foot in the Cape Flats, the area where the so-called Cape Coloreds had been forcibly resettled to implement segregation.

In the week that followed, the assassin's motives were asserted to have been quite different from those the students had taken for granted. He was a madman, nothing else. And nothing more. In a few days Tsafendas's tapeworm had become famous nationwide. The illusory parasite had been the invisible giver of orders: part of a plot, indeed, but a plot for which no one was responsible. Whatever political elements there may have been in Tsafendas's statements to the police were not made known to the public. Barely any attention was given to the fact that he was of mixed parentage. The worm spoke more strongly to the imagination of the public. This suited the authorities well; the country of apartheid was not sick, only the unfortunate Greek.

In October the judge presiding over the trial of Tsafendas declared the accused was not fit to plead. He could not judge this man, he said, "anymore than I can judge a dog." A dog? Demitrios Tsafendas was declared unfit to stand trial and dispatched to the prison on Robben Island.

The attack on Verwoerd meant as much for South Africa as the assassination of John Kennedy had for the United States. It was seen as a break with the past, a loss of innocence, a word writ large on the wall. But what, actually, had taken place? Was it really just a chance event, the deed of a disturbed individual, a madman?

Nothing in South Africa is simple or untouched by racial awareness and racial tensions, not even madness. Or so I came to think later. Many aspects of the events of that day in September were to engrave themselves on my memory. First, there was the question of color. In general, Tsafendas was spoken of simply as Greek. But the notes taken by the doctors in Hamburg had been careless in one respect only: it was his father who had been Cretan and his mother a black

Mozambican—not, as they had said, the other way around. More striking still: Tsafendas's victim, Hendrik Verwoerd, was also the son of an immigrant.

Verwoerd was an outsider in Africa, a Hollander, just like me. The assault had been a confrontation between two immigrants. One half–South African had murdered another half–South African. The answer to many questions lay hidden in those discrepant "halves."

Hendrik Frensch Verwoerd was born in Amsterdam, in a house on Jacob van Lennep Quay. His mother was Frisian; his father was from South Holland. In 1903, when Hendrik was just two years old, the family migrated to the Cape. The Anglo-Boer War had just ended. Wilhelm Verwoerd, the father, like many others in Holland, had been much moved by the battle for freedom fought by the Afrikaners, members of a "brother-nation," brave descendants of the Dutch who had been defeated and humiliated by the British. The fate of these kinsfolk who had established themselves at the foot of the African continent would continue to attract emigrants from the Netherlands for generations. The elder Verwoerd was a carpenter by trade, but his ambition was to mount the pulpit as a dominie, a clergyman of the Dutch Reformed Church. It was an ambition he never fulfilled. In the end he rose to be no more than a lay reader and a catechist. Driven into extreme poverty during the second decade of the century, Wilhelm became a hawker of Calvinistic texts and journals in the remoter districts of the Orange Free State.

His son Hendrik grew up with the High Dutch translation of the Bible, the *Statenbijbel*. Until 1919, when he went to Stellenbosch University in the Cape, he spoke Dutch, not Afrikaans (South African Dutch), at home, although he was much influenced by the anti-British sentiments of the Afrikaner circles in which his family moved. In the course of his parliamentary career his origins would become something of a delicate issue for him, something he preferred to play down. It was not only the opposition that grumbled that he was not a true South African; even among some of his own party, the Afrikaner Nationalists, he remained "the Hollander." Or worse still: the *uitlander*. The foreigner.

Young Verwoerd was exceptionally ambitious. Ostensibly he went to Stellenbosch to study theology and psychology. Soon, however, he was immersed in political matters, especially those involving white poverty and the "race question." Appointed a university lecturer in psychology before his twenty-third birthday, he remained primarily concerned about the future of the "Volk," and the developing Afrikaner Nationalist movement. At that time agricultural failure was driving Afrikaners from the country's interior into the more urbanized Cape peninsula in a pauperized state; inevitably they were compelled to live in the closest proximity with the Cape Colored population. To many Afrikaners, Verwoerd among them, that could only mean national degeneration. In the early 1920s he visited the mixed suburbs of Cape Town, places like District Six. Scandalized by what he saw, he wrote in a university journal about this unhappy state of affairs: "Often one finds colored and white families under one roof.

No wonder that young Afrikaners see no objection to marrying their former little playmates."

Colored or black playmates, of course.

The migrant is an uncertain and incomplete man. He lives in an inveterate state of unease. The ultimate measure of his success is the extent to which he manages to adapt himself to the new circumstances in which he finds himself. But to what could those who are known as "basters"—half-castes—like Demitrios Tsafendas, adapt? Their color was a mark they could not escape, an inheritance they could not leave behind. Why, I used to wonder as a schoolboy, were people of mixed racial origin always given names that sounded like an illness: *métique,* mulatto, half-blood, creole, bastard? To these terms was added the one preferred by Prime Minister Verwoerd: Cape Colored. All nonwhites in South Africa were condemned to live in a no-man's-land, one that might be just around the corner from us. But to those who were the product of racial mixing there clung a special sense of shame, of scandal, a measure of self-hatred, confusion, and anxiety that Tsafendas would experience as a fault line running right through his own body.

And Verwoerd?

His biographer says that he was "the greatest gift the Netherlands gave to South Africa in the twentieth century." No success was denied him in the course of his career. He was an academic, then editor in chief of the Afrikaner Nationalist daily *Die Transvaler,* party leader, senator; he always aligned himself with well-spoken, upright, pious, respectable Afrikaners. One can easily see in his success the typical migrant's ambition to better himself; those who were like him—ex-European, ex-Dutch—found their own condition bettered by Verwoerd's grand embrace of racial discrimination.

In 1950, two years after the Nationalist Party first came to power, Verwoerd was made minister for native affairs. He inherited a system of state-supported racial discrimination, limiting African employment and African ownership of property and forbidding mixed-race "relations" and marriage. But in the 1950s and subsequently during Verwoerd's tenure the system was translated into the elaborate, ever more strictly enforced system of apartheid, which had as its chief aim the separation of the whites of the poorer suburbs from their colored and black fellow countrymen. The goal was to establish an immovable barrier between white and black. Verwoerd was given unlimited power over the black population: in effect he became their dictator. Nobody dared to remind him of his roots, however fond of pickled herring he secretly continued to be. In 1958 he became prime minister. Until his death eight years later he remained the Moses of the Afrikaner tribe.

Nobody questioned his leadership. Most Afrikaners felt that the talented Verwoerd was in direct touch with both their forefathers and a transcendental realm above. He had brought his adopted people to their promised land. But did he really understand them? Enlightened members of the party complained in private that only a Hollander could have thought up his all-consuming and rigid version of apartheid. His interpretation was too hard, too inflexible, and devoted to principle in putting policy into effect. This immigrant's son had not "grown up with the inheritance of his people," or so it was whispered. He took too little account of history or indeed of the colored people, who at one time, albeit in a halfhearted manner, had been offered the prospect of belonging to a "brown Afrikanerdom."

Emigration was an experience I, too, had undergone. My father left Leiden, in the Netherlands, for South Africa in 1956. Six months later—shortly after my ninth birthday—the rest of us followed him. The break with our country of origin was irreparable. Within a couple of years distant Holland became nothing more than a cliché. South Africa—Cape Town—was now my home, yet it was a country in which no one appeared to feel at home.

Our local grocer was also a migrant of a kind: he was always looked on as an outsider, a "coolie," a "curry guzzler." His forefathers had been shipped to the country by the Dutch East India Company. He could speak four languages and was the only person in the neighborhood who read books rather than the comic strips in the newspapers. Bent over the Koran, in the half-light of his shop, he became my own image of a learned man. His shop smelled of *samosas,* of *bredies, sosaties,* and other Cape Malay dishes. The faith he followed appealed in equal measure to my nostrils, my stomach, and my understanding. I visited the Claremont Main Road Mosque, near a slaughterer's yard, about a half-hour walk from our house, and was received there in a friendly manner. I went to the Awwal Mosque on Dorp Street, on a rise above the city, where the imam repeatedly invited me to come in. Every time I did so the carpets and multicolored glow of light astonished me anew. I also made my way to the Shrine (*kramaat*) of Sheikh Yussuf of Macassar, a sacred, sweet-smelling place lost amid the windblown dunes of False Bay.

I knew next to nothing about Islam. But it seemed to me to have adapted itself in a more comely fashion to the harsh realties of southern Africa than the Dutch Reformed or Anglican churches. From about the time I was twelve the faith began to exercise an irresistible attraction over me, both because in my eyes it was so bound up with book learning— preserved and transmitted in a strange, attractive orthography—and because of what I perceived to be its sensuousness. The frigidly ascetic Bible classes of the Anglicans and Methodists offered nothing comparable to the recurring resonant cries from the minaret, to the *riempie-sny,* a feast celebrated with banners and fluttering citrus leaves, and to the ceremonies of the *khalifah,* or *ratiep.* My father disapproved of the last particularly: the beating drums, the dancing of those dagger-brandishing men, and then at the high point of the ritual, skewers run through cheek or lip, swords slashing at bellies, bare feet walking on burning coals—everything wonderfully without blood or blister. *Inshallah! Allahu-Akbar!*

In the early 1960s the racially mixed suburb of Cape Town where we lived was, in effect, done away with. Our Cape Colored neighbors disappeared. I was about thirteen years old when it happened. They had gone against their will:

everyone knew that. Everyone remained silent. Our scholarly
grocer who had done so much to arouse my interest in Islam
was compelled to trek along with all the others who had
something "wrong" with them. The neighborhood bar was
closed, then knocked down. I could no longer go with my
sketchbook to draw the drunks who made a racket on the
stoep of the bar or stretched themselves out to sleep on a patch
of empty ground nearby. The mosque was left standing—it
was consecrated ground—but the believers, the people whose
mosque it had been, were removed from our district. It all
happened very quietly. I cannot remember their departure,
only a vague feeling of unease and the question: Where had
they gone? Not long afterward the answer became clear.
They had been taken to the Cape Flats, many miles away. Our
neighborhood held its peace.

How many South Africans were forced out of their cities
during the fifties and sixties? Three million? Four million,
some say—between 12 and 15 percent, anyway, of the total
population of the country. And for what reason? The differences between the "poor white" Afrikaners and the coloreds,
especially, were not all that easy to make out, on either side of
the color line. Both groups spoke the same language and felt
the same longing for a recognition of the wrongs done to
them in the past. But what a child could not understand was
this: the war between races is always fought most fiercely
when the differences between them are least apparent.

"Borderline cases," my mother used to say. And of the
awful fate that had befallen such cases she added, with a sense

of shock and compassion that made a deep impression on me (all the more so because my father did not share her sentiments): No wonder there have been so many suicides and murders.

Some borderline cases did their best to hide their condition. At the age of fifteen I fell in love with a classmate. Her name was Susan. She was crazy about the ballet. She had a small snub nose and bit her nails to the quick, so that the tips of her fingers swelled out above them. And every Sunday evening she steamed her hair and ironed it flat. Otherwise the crinkle would have been too obvious and she would have been exposed to even more teasing than she already had to endure. I found all her characteristics attractive: her little cries, the break in her voice, the fact that she sometimes chose to read books for pleasure. Also that she gave dancing lessons to black children in the slums.

She had set up a dance class in the Cape Flats. For months she and her group practiced to put on a performance in public. I felt compelled to attend the first night, which was also to be the last. That Friday evening I set off on my own in a bus that took me to the "nonwhite" suburbs. Soon we reached a part of town where the little houses began to look more and more alike and the bus stops grew farther and farther apart. There were few streetlights. I got off the bus and began walking in search of the hall. Turning a corner I came on a group of *skollies*—Cape Colored toughs—who were having a go at each other. I took refuge behind a hedge. They had their jackets folded over their left arms. Blades glittered in their right hands. The brawl was over in a moment. One of the figures lay where he had fallen.

I ran. The impenetrable darkness notwithstanding, I did not dare to ask anyone the way. On reaching the hall, I found it packed with enthusiastic parents and relatives. I was the only white person present, I believe, but no one paid any attention to me. The atmosphere was festive; first there was some singing, then came the performance. At the end of it I went up on the platform, in full view of everyone, and got from Susan the kiss I had dreamed of for so long.

A few months later, a year before our final examinations, her parents took her out of school. Her departure from the class was swift and surrounded by questions, rumors, silences. In haste the family left for Australia.

It was around this time I began to read the newspapers regularly. The *Cape Times* kept the score: every weekend about two hundred stabbings took place around the city. Though no special notice was taken of the fact, we were trapped in a kind of low-intensity civil war.

It is impossible to describe how deep the sense of mutual estrangement was. Differences of language, faith, or race were only the most obvious indicators of a chronic, irremediable lack of civil cohesion. Little effort was made by most urban whites to cultivate any sense of common human decency. They had no idea that the social attitudes they took for granted had been learned: painstakingly inculcated and acquired. It is a mistake to imagine they were brought up merely to discriminate against others on the grounds of color.

The repulsion they felt was more profound. They had been taught to feel hate, a hate that gnawed at them like the hunger of an animal waiting to be fed.

I felt hatred too, but my repugnance was focused on everything that was or pertained to being white. During my final year at school I seldom went to a pub or party with my classmates. Their recreation involved rugby matches or boasts about their feats in the surf. Beachboys in the making. As soon as I was old enough to go about on my own, my inclinations drew me toward the inner city. There I found quite a different Africa from the one we were told about in the classroom. In the Muslim Upper Cape, on the slopes immediately above the downtown area, and in District Six, far from the teenyboppers and the claustrophobia of the white suburbs, a world persisted beyond the crazy racial exclusions that bound our lives elsewhere.

At the age of eighteen I moved to Woodstock, a neighborhood in the center of town, close to District Six, a notoriously rundown area. It felt freer than other places; it had retained something of the amorphous melting pot Verwoerd had worked so hard to eradicate. Racial integration had gone further here, and was more difficult to undo, than anywhere else. That it was a slum, a filthy and violent place, went without saying.

During the nineteenth century the population of District Six had consisted chiefly of liberated slaves or their descendants, transported to the Cape from Java, Malaya, and elsewhere by the Dutch East India Company. By the turn of the century they had been joined by immigrants and refugees from Europe, including about seven thousand Jews from the Baltic provinces of the Russian empire, British soldiers discharged at the end of the Anglo-Boer War, Boers bankrupted by that same war, and black migrant laborers from the colony's eastern frontier. Ten or fifteen years later the district was regarded as a kind of transit zone: those who succeeded moved away from it. The whites established themselves in the suburbs to the south of Table Mountain and along the coastline of Sea Point. Modern transportation helped: without it, this dispersal of population over the entire Cape would have been impossible. The people who were left behind, within walking distance of the city center, were dependent on employment in the harbor area and the factories around it. They were paid by the hour or day. When Verwoerd came to power the overwhelming majority of them were colored, a warning (to him) of the racial mixing that white poverty inevitably brought in its wake.

Alas, this area, too, was to be destroyed by the oppressive power of the state, not to speak of the constriction of the heart that was both precondition and consequence of government policy. District Six was regarded by the Nationalist Party as a "black spot" disfiguring the city. On 11 February 1966, the minister for community affairs announced the end of the neighborhood. It was to be completely flattened. The inhabitants would be driven en masse to the Cape Flats. They would have to manage there as best they could, far from their work, from the shelter of Table Mountain, and from the streets familiar to them. Dumped in a region tormented by dust and wind, they were left to their fate.

•

In the winter of 1966, after the murdered Verwoerd had been succeeded by a much-feared former minister of justice, Balthasar Vorster, Demitrios Tsafendas was transferred from Robben Island to Pretoria Central prison. He was placed in a cell next to death row and forgotten. Those who had hoped the murder of Verwoerd might be followed by a revolt against apartheid or that such an event might shake the Afrikaners from their complacency and racial delusions were shown to have been deceiving themselves. Dreamers all. Within the narrow coterie of their own kind, the whites clung to each other even more closely than before. Any attempt at mixing with the people with whom I had always felt myself most at ease—the Cape Coloreds—was automatically suspect in their eyes. I was frozen out, as were others like me.

Six months after the assassination I walked into the consulate of the Netherlands, on Strand Street, and asked—in English—for a passport. They barely lifted their heads to look at me. Nor did they notice that officially I had no existence in South Africa. In order to escape compulsory military service, I had never registered for an identity card, which all South Africans were required to carry. I wandered around as best I could and paid no taxes, carrying no "white pass." The passport was issued forthwith.

I arrived in Europe in the spring of 1968. I had burned my bridges behind me. I felt optimistic, wholly unprepared for the great thirst that awaited me, the nostalgia I would feel for the future I had left behind.

How often, over the next twenty years, did I dream that I was back in South Africa? Euphoric dreams, they were, though always uncertain in their outcome. And then in the summer of 1989, I came back.

The morning of my return, I was woken by a radio quacking busily in Afrikaans. This was no dream. All night the notorious Cape southeaster had been blowing, shaking the window frames with its great hands. I pulled the bedclothes aside, dressed hastily, and made for the botanical gardens in the center of town, the Company Gardens, as they are called, after the Dutch East India Company, which established the country's first white settlement here, directly under Table Mountain.

Were things as they used to be? The trees were tenderly lit by a languid sun. Beneath the trees were some small tables. A dark-skinned man was mowing the grass. On the back of his orange overalls were the letters C.C.C.—Cape City Council. Surely no place on earth was pleasanter. Returning after so long an absence, I discovered, meant that I had to do everything all over again. I went through the suburbs known to me, uphill and down: toward the mountain, through the city center, down to the docks. I could have found my way blindfolded. The streets were empty; the sun's rays reached across to the booming sea. From a distance I could hear the call of the muezzin. I got on a double-decker bus going toward Sea Point. It too was empty. When we turned a corner, going away from the docks, there once more, where it had always been, yet seemingly brand-new too, was a service station with gas pumps. As the bus went by, the little structure appeared to reconstruct itself from the past, swiftly yet complete in every detail.

In a lane next to it stood two colored people, a man and a woman. Both were in rags. The man's movements were slow but purposeful. With his clenched fist he struck the woman in the middle of her face. She fell, struggled upright, and screamed soundlessly. He leaned toward her again, bending his head toward her breast. Then he pulled her blouse over her head and tore it in two. She crumpled against a wall. No passing car honked. No one started toward her. It was as if a breeze had moved through the branches, nothing more.

Home again.

Later I took the train to the southern suburbs and the beaches of False Bay. It was not long since the signs on the station walls saying WHITES ONLY had been removed. Older yet brighter patches of ochre paint showed where the signs used to be. The train itself was still divided more or less along racial lines. Coloreds and whites were to be found in first class; second class did not exist. Third class was packed—blacks sat on the bare wooden seats.

We ambled through the suburbs. The window was open, letting in the warm air. Opposite me sat an elderly English-speaking woman, soft-skinned, smelling of lavender. She was visibly nervous. At every stop she breathed with relief once it became clear that the noisy Cape Colored throngs were rushing into other cars. The little station buildings, the fences and flower beds, looked orphaned, uncared-for, as if they had not been touched since my departure.

The crowds grew thicker as we left the white suburbs behind. With the abolishing of racial segregation on the beaches, the entire colored population of the Cape Flats seemed to be streaming toward sections of the coast previously forbidden to them. At Deep River station scores of youngsters ran jubilantly ahead of their parents. Every time the train began to move, excited children sprinted alongside it, making daredevil attempts to get on board while their friends struggled to hold the sliding doors open for them. Of the conductor there was no sign.

On an impulse I got off the train at the beach resort of Muizenberg. It had always struck me as a place with a certain British-colonial aspect. Now its British reticence had vanished. It was given over instead to what looked like a kind of carnival. An endlessly variegated crowd had taken possession of the beach. The families I had earlier seen rushing to board the train were joined by all those who had made their way to the coast in decrepit cars, minibuses, and coaches.

I walked along the promenade. Was all this true? Was I seeing correctly? During the sixties a rigorous color bar had been enforced here. If your skin looked too dark you could be told to take down your swimming trunks, so that the paleness or otherwise of your backside could be examined. I'd hardly ever gone to this beach then—not so much in protest against the rules and the ludicrous boundaries they protected but because I felt such distaste for the California-style surfers putting on a display of their special kind of White Power. Now I wandered among thousands of people of whom I seemed to be the only one who remembered those distant days.

How does one liberate a beach? This beach had been liberated.

In clothes of all styles and hues, as if taken from a children's dress-up basket, the crowds sported in the water and along the promenade; they tumbled about on the grass and in the old-fashioned amusement park. They played soccer with tennis balls, cricket with bits of driftwood; they dragged fishing boats out of the waves, boasted and shouted over the catch, bargained and argued. The air was heavy and sultry. Gulls veered and hung in a breeze smelling strongly of seaweed. I walked back and forth, fascinated by the animation, the noise, the sense of ordinariness that for so long had been unthinkable.

Many of the older people wore white hats and shawls and white, knitted fezlike caps. Most of the youngsters had been born since my departure from the country. I did not see a single face I knew, yet everywhere I recognized the familiar Malay features and Arabian eyes of people who had been driven without apology out of their homes. And here I was among them all: ghost-pale, long-nosed, tremulous as a hare.

Within a matter of days I had begun working in the National Library—an imposing edifice, a replica of the Fitzwilliam Museum in Cambridge—which stands near Cape Town's parliamentary building, the Supreme Court, the once-dreaded police headquarters on Caledon Square, and the Anglican Cathedral. I had by then paid my inevitable visits to what used to be my family home, as well as to the factory in which my father had worked as an instrument maker. I had also succeeded in getting myself mugged twice: the first time coming out of an ebulliently low-life disco (The Base) at about three in the morning; the second, more frighteningly, on a train, in broad daylight, at the point of a knife. "We only want your money, man," explained the child who held the blade directly to my stomach. He and his friends were all children, long-legged boys with muddy eyes and fuzz on their cheeks. I pulled a few crumpled notes out of my pocket, but they were not to be so easily satisfied. "We *really* want your money, man," hissed the knife carrier, gesturing at my navel with his weapon. I began to disgorge everything I had in my pockets. Coins bounced about on the floor. A general scrabbling, grabbing, and swearing followed. The people in the neighboring sections of the car did not move. It all seemed to go on for an eternity. Then came a change in the rhythm of the train, the sound of brakes, a flickering of light and shadow. We were entering Salt River station. Doors opened noisily. My besiegers turned, hesitated, and made off down the platform. What I most wanted to do was to light a cigarette. But they had taken my matches too.

Later, in a dimly lit office in the city's main station, I reported the incident to the railway police. I did not understand why I went to the trouble of doing it. For the sake of the statistics? "*Yirra,* those blerrie buggers!" said the policeman to whom I told my tale. "Why don't you carry a gun?"

From that world, from the world outside, the library hardly offered a refuge. Each time I entered it I remembered how impressed I had been when I first visited the place as a seventeen-year-old matriculant. Its lofty cupola, which seemed to float in midair when you looked up at it, served in effect as a whispering gallery or echo chamber. The turn of a page, the faintest murmur, was transformed into an unforgiving crackle. A cough was like rifle shot. Sitting there, pretending to be an adult, I would concentrate on keeping as still as I could, lest I disturb the others. Now, in another chamber, I bent for days on end over card indexes and copies of newspapers preserved on microfiche, scavenging and gathering material by instinct, basketsful of material, hoping that I would find a use for it all—though I could not imagine what that use might turn out to be. What would I do with the "Report of the Commission of Enquiry into Secret Organisations" (1965)? Or a study entitled *Possession by Spirits among the Zulus*? Or the newspaper article headlined "Bantus to Be

Greeted in Their Own Manner" (1966), which reported an authoritative ruling by the central government that white civil servants were under no circumstances to shake hands with blacks?

The past unfolded before me incoherently, yet in a manner that swept away all rationalizations. "You knew it was happening, you read the newspapers and heard the rumors, didn't you?" Again and again the ugliness of that period thrust itself into my consciousness: the stupidity, the lies, the violence, the censorship—from the massacre at Sharpeville in 1960 and even before then too: the grotesquely obscene "immorality" trials of Dutch Reformed dominies caught in garages with their colored maids or of farmers spied on in the open veld with their female domestics and duly brought to reckoning before the courts. With a rising gorge I deliberately made my way through a four months' sampling of issues of *Die Burger,* the Nationalist Party daily newspaper in the Cape, from 1 January 1960 to the end of April: 120 days under Verwoerd's premiership, chosen more or less at random. What I found was a caricature of a country, my country, sick, disordered, petrified.

From time to time, fleeing from the nauseating facts I was dredging up, I would go out into the Company Gardens. Or I would sit on the terrace and drink tea, trying to contain my anger. Seagulls raised their cries among the magnolias. Table Mountain was always visible through the leaves of the trees. More than a thousand meters high, too broad to see around, it was a theatrical yet ever-silent witness of what passed below. So many important events in South African history had taken place in this precinct: demonstrations, marches, processions.

Murder, too. Among the documents awaiting me was the 1966 "Report of the Commission of Enquiry into the Death of the Late Honourable Dr. Hendrik Frensch Verwoerd," which gave an account of the assassination, together with the official and supposedly final version of the life of Demitrios Tsafendas. I paid my money and carried away a photocopy of the report in its entirety. I had no idea then how much extensive and revealing material about Tsafendas I would find elsewhere. Nor did I guess that seven years later, after several further visits to the country and many bureaucratic delays, I would at last be allowed to meet him face-to-face.

Born in 1918, Demitrios Tsafendas could remember nothing of the first house he had lived in, on the Rua Andrade Corvo in Lourenço Marques (now Maputo). He spent no more than a year there.

His father, Michaelis Tsafandakis, who was Cretan by birth, had migrated from the Egyptian port of Alexandria to the highveld city of Pretoria in the Transvaal. Early in 1916 he moved to Mozambique to take a job with an Italian firm of marine engineers. He was a striking young man with a heavy moustache and a lengthy stride—like an ostrich's, some said. He soon won a reputation as a hardworking but excitable man. The Africans who worked under him looked on him with some fear. Within the local Greek community he was respected for his independence of mind. People put his brusque, inflammable temperament down to his Cretan origins. That he employed two black maids in his house on Rua Andrade excited no particular comment. With one of them—the seventeen-year-old Amelia Williams—he shared his bed. She was a girl of mixed European and African descent. In the tropics it was more or less the order of the day for a single man to keep a concubine. Everyone assumed that Michaelis would eventually marry a fellow Greek.

The house was semidetached. The neighbors saw Amelia going about her chores and working in the garden. She watered and fed the chickens, humming with a strange intensity as she did so. She went barefoot and wore a multicolored cotton skirt like that worn by the women in neighboring Swaziland. Over her shoulders she wore a light shawl. The rumor was that Michaelis had his hands full keeping her under control.

In 1917 she became pregnant. She spent some time with her family in Namaacha, a district on the border between Mozambique and Swaziland. She returned in midsummer. In January she gave birth to a boy.

Michaelis was confronted with a dilemma. The child was his firstborn son, but marriage to Amelia was out of the question. He allowed the child to be registered in his name in the office of the local Administraçao Civil. The entry reads: "Demitrios, 14 January 1918, son of Amelia Williams and Miguel Tsafandakis." Some months later an Orthodox priest was brought down from Johannesburg to baptize Demitrios. His godfather—Michaelis's good friend Perandonakis, also a Cretan—bore the costs of the ceremony. Amelia did not attend it. By then relations between her and Michaelis had been severed.

The house next door was occupied by Anthony Maw, who later became honorary consul for Greece in Lourenço Marques. After Amelia Williams's departure, Maw and his wife wondered how their neighbor would cope. The baby was unmistakably a half-blood. To the young English couple this meant he was bound to become a shackle around his father's legs, but they kept their opinion to themselves. In effect, the baby was being brought up by the other servant girl.

One day in spring Maw leaned over the hedge that divided the two gardens. He could see the maid sitting among the bougainvilleas with the baby in her lap. The father stood nearby. Tsafandakis—who had always been on the sturdy side—had grown stout. The two men fell into conversation. Michaelis spoke English only hesitantly, sometimes in cryptic fashion. In three months' time he would turn thirty-five, he confided to his neighbor. His family, which lived in Crete and in Egypt, was in the process of searching for a bride for him. Maw remarked that a young European wife would not find it agreeable to be burdened with an illegitimate child of that kind. After some roundabout small talk Michaelis confessed that he wanted to send his little son to Alexandria. There he could be brought up by Michaelis's mother. The problem was that Michaelis did not know anyone who would be able to accompany the baby to Egypt.

By this time Maw's wife had joined in the conversation. It so happened that she knew someone who would shortly be going to Athens. By steamship, through the Suez Canal. She promised to find out more.

Among the Greeks this was quite a common way of dealing with such matters. Many grandparents in effect brought up their grandchildren.

The widow Katerina Tsafandakis fetched her grandson Demitrios from the boat in Port Said. He was to spend his next six years in Alexandria. That is to say, his earliest memories were of the cosmopolitan cultural life of the eastern Mediterranean. At home he spoke Greek; in the street, Arabic. His first impressions were colored by Mediterranean light, a confusion of warehouses and bazaars, the heat and crowds of the small lanes near the docks. The great commercial city looked at the same time east and west; though one window was open on the unstable world of the Levant, the city still lay within the British sphere of influence and its closely knit Greek colony dated back to ancient times.

Katerina lived on the top floor of a house on Rue Toussoum Pasha, not far from the pale-red building of the Banco di Roma. Around the corner was Place Mohammed Ali, the biggest square in the town center, where the colonial court buildings and the cotton exchange were to be found. Toward evening the noisy chatter of Alexandrian sparrows could be heard from the trees. The sparrows, which landed in great numbers on the terrace of the house, fascinated Demitrios from an early age. During the hot summers he slept on the terrace and closed his eyes to the rustle of the birds. In the mornings, at first light, he was woken by the voice of the imam, carried from the mosque all over the neighborhood.

Grandmother Tsafandakis gave him the pet name Mimis. She took him with her to the market, to the Anglican church in the Place Mohammed Ali, and to the cathedral of St. Saba, the seat of the Orthodox patriarch. Later she took him to the English puppet theater in the city, which was particularly popular among Greek children. For the rest he would spend the whole day dressed in a trailing djellaba, playing at being a little Arab boy.

From his grandmother the little boy learned to identify the electric trams that ran in an elaborate network all over the city. Mimis surprised her by the quickness with which he learned to recognize the different lines. He pointed out to her their symbols: the green lozenge that marked the tramline to the south, the red half-moon of the Ragheb Pasha line, the white star, red circle, and green leaf of the other lines.

Sometimes Katrina worried about her grandson. He was seldom ill-behaved, but often she thought him too withdrawn. He was uneasy with children his own age and kept to himself. She stuffed him with sultanas, raisins, and dates, which he loved.

His father visited Egypt a few times. The sea route along the coast of East Africa was much traveled and Michaelis's contacts with Greek shipowners made trips easy to arrange. Mimis looked forward to these visits, though they were too irregular for him to get to know his father. The little presents he received from him he found strange: wood carvings of an unfamiliar kind, a little handheld thumb piano made out of a gourd, with keys of bent steel.

By this time Michaelis was a married man. The young Marika, who had come to him from the Greek community in Port Said, accompanied him on these journeys. As Demitrios grew up, he began to look on Marika as his mother: a mother at a distance. In remote Lourenço Marques he eventually acquired from her a little sister and brother—Evangelina and Victor. But the children remained mere names to him and Lourenço Marques was a phantom, a dream town found only in stories.

Mimis had to go on living with Katerina.

When he could not fall asleep she would recite to him long passages from the *Erotokritas,* an epic that she knew by heart, just as the Muslim youngsters could recite from the Koran for an hour at a time.

They lay together on the sofa next to the open window. The evenings were smoky and restless. The Cretan verses comforted him like candy.

There were questions the child could not ask her but of whose nature he was fully aware. Demitrios had the feeling that something was being kept from him. For reasons he could not understand he was at a disadvantage. The circumstances of his birth remained unspoken, unknown to him.

By the time he was seven years old he was a quiet but outwardly contented boy. He was free to wander as he wished through the town. He rambled about the docks, attracted by their hubbub and by the ships on their way to Tripoli or Heraklion. He spent the midday hours on the Corniche, the broad road along the coast, from which you could see the fort on Qayt Bay. It was the only trace of the ancient lighthouse still standing, or so Katerina had once told him. In the Greek quarter of the town, behind St. Saba Cathedral, Mimis was a well-known figure. Only Ras el Tin, the Turkish district near the Cape of Figs, was forbidden territory. Disorder was brewing there.

The uprising of the Arabs against the British regime made a great impression on him. All the doors of the house were bolted. There were riots in the street. The nationalists set fire to the covered market where he bought his sherbets. From the terrace of his house he looked down on the English and Australian troops as they formed up and suddenly opened fire. With salvo upon salvo they drove the rebels out of the district. When his grandmother saw him sitting there she dragged him indoors. It was the only time he could remember hearing her curse.

By 1925 Katerina had grown too frail to look after him. Mimis had become too much of a handful for her. In the course of that year his father arrived. The plan was that he would take the boy south, back to the promised land of Lourenço Marques. Mimis had grown into a slender youngster, with a narrow face surmounted by an uncontrollable bush of kinky hair.

Things had gone well for Michaelis, whose family, for some time resident in the Britannia Hotel, was now living in an apartment on the top floor of a large whitewashed building in a pleasant part of town, at 24 July Avenue. In it there would be enough room for them all: for Marika, Michaelis, and their two children, Evangelina and Victor. Another girl, Helena, soon followed. Michaelis wished to do his best for Mimis, too. He had to go to school and learn the local languages. Marika had objected to his arrival, but she had been overruled. The domestic staff was expanded to include an extra maid. For the eight-year-old Demitrios it was difficult at first to accept the change from a Mediterranean to an African style of life. He could understand nobody outside the family. He missed the familiar sounds and the comfortable neighborhood of his grandmother's house. He was sent to school in a Portuguese mission in the city and was placed in the lowest grade. The white children spoke in a harsh, clipped manner, as if giving orders. The blacks shouted. Even nature and natural events seemed loud and abrupt here. In the evenings it looked as if the sun died in a single moment behind the hills. In the mornings it stood up as if with a clap above the horizon. There was no sense of intermediacy, no dawn or dusk.

This absence of nuance was visible everywhere. In Alexandria the Greeks were a respected minority, protected by the British, even after Egypt declared itself independent in 1922. Here, below the equator, prejudices were much sharper. The Anglo-Saxon and Portuguese way of doing things emphasized distinctions within the colony. Race and class reinforced each other. The Greek merchants, tobacco planters, and workers were looked down on, along with "coolies and local savages." The Greeks in Mozambique clung together in their own community, seeking to preserve what they could of the culture of their motherland. Michaelis Tsafandakis knew less about local politics than he did about developments in Athens. And in general he was less well informed and educated than his wife.

Demitrios was not a part of his father's milieu, but then where did he really belong? In his new surroundings he missed the intimacy, warmth, and mutual trust he had enjoyed with Katerina. Whether or not he would ever be able to fit in would depend largely on Marika.

She was an intelligent woman, born to a worldly family in Port Said. Next to the corpulent Michaelis, she looked small, with an athletic figure and an urgent way of going about things. She had a pockmarked but agreeable face. A thick braid hung down almost to her waist. She spoke French and a little Italian and had rapidly learned Portuguese and English. At the time of Demitrios's arrival she was just twenty-three years old, seventeen years younger than her husband.

In her heart she looked on Michaelis's love child as an intruder and feared that his father would favor him over her own children. Nevertheless she had decided to treat him no differently from the others. It was clear to her that Demitrios had to be taken in hand. He could not read or write, he knew nothing of Greek history. He seemed to have been left to his own devices in Egypt.

Mimis soon came to admire his new mother. Even if she remained somewhat distant in manner, she gave him treats from her kitchen and was good at telling stories. She told him about de Lesseps and the building of the Suez Canal, about the Acropolis and the Orthodox saints. After dinner she would bring thick books to the table and read to the children. She had a gramophone on which she played European records. And what perhaps impressed him most about her was that she had set up a small shrine in an alcove near the bedrooms. (There was no Greek Orthodox church in Lourenço

Marques.) The family paid a formal visit to that confined, darkened space last thing at night, every night. Little oil-lamps she had brought with her from Port Said remained alight twenty-four hours a day.

The flames threw a wonderful sparkle over the icons. It kept alive in Demitrios's mind the places he used to visit with his grandmother in his Alexandrian days. Evening after evening the chilly golden saints and fathers of the church stared flickeringly down at him. It was as if the air itself were aflame yet still preserved an eternal coolness of its own.

Outside, the heat was overwhelming. For six months or longer Marika stood by her resolution not to make a distinc-tion between her children and the newcomer; then, all at once, it shattered. It was clear to her that Michaelis had become greatly attached to the boy, even more so than she had feared. He paid much less attention to the younger children. And then there was the climate! She complained that her head of hair was much too heavy to bear. She wanted to cut it short, because she suffered from severe recurring headaches, especially now, in the summer. It felt as if her skull were being constantly pulled at. But Michaelis forbade her to cut her hair. Sometimes he could behave tyrannically toward her.

"Your son has been messing with your things," she would call out maliciously to him. *Your* son.

Mimis was a nuisance, a burden to her. He disrupted the harmonious life of the family. Evangelina and little Victor, especially, suffered under his teasing and changes of mood. Punishing him did not help. When Michaelis scolded him he would sit in the kitchen and stare silently in front of him. Or he would fall into a rage. Outside the house he was treated like some kind of primitive. And he behaved like one, too: unpredictable and threatening.

Another six months passed, and the fights between Mimis and Marika were a daily occurrence. Michaelis found their quarreling insufferable. When Mimis turned nine he was sent to a boarding school for white, English-speaking children in the Union of South Africa. Many children from middle-class families of continental European background went to such places and managed well enough. The educational system in the Transvaal was more developed than anything to be found in the Portuguese colony. His command of English would no doubt soon improve.

So, for the first time in his life, Mimis found himself living far from the coast and the smell of the sea. The bleak little Transvaal town of Middelburg lay four hundred kilometers west of Lourenço Marques and about a hundred kilometers east of Pretoria.

He was placed in Nelson House Hostel, a large, elongated, colonial-style building with a shady verandah and a neglected garden in front. The pupils in this hostel came almost exclusively from Greek and Portuguese families, a group that was kept together partly but not entirely because of their backwardness in English. On their arrival, all students of foreign background were put back a year or two. Stimulated by the differences in lifestyle between themselves and the other boys, they developed a camaraderie of their own. They also had the advantage of being able to speak in secret tongues, and they generally did well in all subjects other than English and Afrikaans. For this they were duly persecuted by the other boys. Everyone looked down on them. The prejudices of the English-speaking townspeople ran no less deep than those of the local Afrikaners. The Portuguese were called "sea kaffirs"; the Greeks were notorious for being untrustworthy. The whites whispered among themselves about the dark practices that went on in the hostel.

"We all knew," one of the Afrikaans-speaking boys from another hostel later recalled, "that sodomy was a common habit in that tightly knit group."

Demitrios was in the same position as the others from Mozambique, and this created a bond between them and him. If he was noticed at all in this group, initially, it was because of the seriousness of his manner. He was strikingly earnest for a boy his age. Another burden on him was his susceptibility to frequent feverish attacks. No one investigated the possibility that these might have been malarial in origin. It was evident that he believed himself to be out of the ordinary. He would speak in a joking, offhand manner to one of the women teachers about his life in Egypt. Later his feelings about the school grew darker. Its ethos stuck in his throat. British ways were stricter and more heavy-handed than those he had known before, either from his father or from his grandmother. He was compelled to take part in sports like cricket of which he understood nothing. If he felt homesick it was not so much for his parents as for his racially mixed companions at the mission school in Lourenço Marques. He missed particularly the voices of the black children. He missed Marika's kitchen maid. The food in the hostel was unpalatable to him: sausages, kippers, oatmeal with too little sugar, mealie porridge.

His greatest pleasure was to go to the automatic candy machine outside Cleggs Cafe in the dorp's main street. Each time he was given his pocket money by Mr. Marindale, the warden of the hostel, he went straight to Cleggs. He fed the machine with the giant British-style copper pennies in use then, with the date of their minting stamped on them: 1921, 1899, 1909. Then the candies came out and he rolled them in his hand.

"Very good. Remarkably good."

That was how he felt then, with his mouth full of chocolate. That was how, a lifetime later—after asking me if I happened to have any chocolate with me—he chose to describe the taste to me.

After a couple of terms in the Transvaal, Mimis still had a limited command of English, but he could speak it freely enough. At the age of twelve or thirteen he was familiar with five languages, but he could speak none of them correctly. His Arabic lay in the past. The same was true of Shangaan, the local African language, which he had learned from the mission-school children. He disliked Afrikaans, which struck him as a language appropriate to the country: one of naked, stony sounds. In Middelburg he dreamed in Greek and woke in English.

By the time he reached the fifth grade he had become the

clown of his peer group, more because of his wild gesticula-
tions than because of anything he said. When he sang Cretan
songs at school concerts, he had the excited, laughing,
applauding audience eating out of his hand. Yet his gesturing
and general appearance also provoked the other boys to tease
and bully him. He was plagued especially by a boy named
Benjamin Levy, whose father was the manager of the Savoy
Hotel in Lourenço Marques. On one occasion the fat Benny,
together with his friend Sammy Schmahmann, kicked him
in the shins in the wasteland beyond the playing fields. Mimis
struck back at them vainly and came away with a bloody
nose.

This was the first time that he heard the expression *colored*
flung at him.

"You're nothing but a lousy colored!" shouted the fat boy.
"A lousy bloody colored."

He at once felt ashamed and humiliated, though he did not
know why. Boer, Briton, Jew, colored—these distinctions had
largely passed him by. His parents were Greek: could there be
anything surprising, then, if his skin was darker than that of
the pale, English-speaking ghosts of the highveld? Nor was
Mimis the only boy with kinky hair in Middelburg Primary
School. But there was no one else whose words were so
twisted and strange. His boasts were always exposed; his fantasies convinced nobody. Whenever he told lies or tried to
cheat at games the others saw through him at once. Only in
eating and in singing did he distinguish himself—the intensity with which he flung himself into both these activities was
beyond measure.

In the hills outside the little town he had discovered some caves. It was a primitive and isolated place, surrounded by strangely formed boulders, some the work of nature, some of men's hands. He spent hours in these caves. Alone. With a candle. Though no icons were to be found there, the place was his shrine.

Twice a year, during the school holidays, he went home by train: for a couple of weeks in the winter and for almost two months in the summer. Marika was happier to see him go than to see him come. In September 1928 she had had another girl, who was baptized Katerina, in honor of the child's grandmother Tsafandakis. In addition to the three girls, Marika had her son, Victor, who was often unwell, to look after. Each time her stepson appeared she became more and more convinced that there was something abnormal about him. He was always acting, putting on a performance. When he thought no one was watching him he would make crazy faces. The full story about Amelia was still hidden from Demitrios, but Marika was not surprised to hear that he was accused by the boys at his school of being a colored. It would have been better for him, she thought, if he had remained in Egypt. In Egypt he would have passed more easily.

Demitrios spent much of his time in the kitchen. He had no real relationship with the other children, except his three-year-old sister. Sometimes he would go into Evangelina's bedroom. He called her Betty Boop, after the little girl in the American cartoon. He explained to Betty Boop how gunpowder worked, and told her he was going to make skyrockets with it. Evangelina understood little of what he was saying, but she enjoyed listening to him. Her brother used words that were strange to her. He spoke of "tuck" when he meant candy and chips; he called bananas "lady's fingers," and brought a bunch of small bananas from the kitchen to show her what a good name that was.

His father, too, was unhappy with the boy's appearance and demeanor. He asked himself why Demitrios was so timid and turned in on himself; so chicken-breasted, skinny, weedy. He had round, girlish shoulders and showed no interest in the activities that kept the other youngsters in the neighborhood busy. At home he was under everyone's feet; when Michaelis took him to his workplace, at the firm of Vucellato, he usually just followed his father about. He liked watching the welders at work, but then he would lose interest. He collected strips of metal from the lathes, played with grindstones and molds.

Michaelis discussed the boy with an old acquaintance, Guillema Conte, who had set up a gym in the city. Señor Conte offered to take the youngster under his wing during the summer months. Demitrios, he said, should learn to box. Then at least he would be able to defend himself if anyone ever called him a "blackie" back in Middelburg. In the years that followed, Mimis went to the gym set up by Conte and his brother fairly often, at first to oblige Michaelis, later because he became interested in the sport.

Jack Dempsey was soon one of his greatest heroes. The other was Buster Keaton.

•

At the beginning of the 1930s the worldwide depression dominated life in southern Africa. Michaelis did not know if he would be able to survive in Mozambique or how he would be able to pay Mimis's fees at the boarding school in Middelburg. Maritime traffic had dwindled. The firm for which he worked was going downhill. Many immigrants to Portuguese East Africa were leaving for the Transvaal, where conditions were a little better. In 1931 Michaelis applied to the South African Department of Immigration and Asiatic Affairs for permission for the children, at least, to be registered as members of the Greek community in Pretoria.

That summer Demitrios returned once again to the family residence. After four years in Middelburg he had got no farther than the sixth grade. The next eighteen months he spent as a student, supposedly, at the Portuguese mission school that he had attended before.

For the most part he simply played truant; he spent his days wherever his fancy took him. At night he rummaged around the apartment. Marika found it hard to cope with his appetite. He ate as much as he could, whenever he could, yet he remained as thin as ever. Was that usual for a boy his age? She did not know. The only thing he really cared for was the gramophone. He said he wanted to learn the piano, but there was no money to buy such a thing for him. He sat with red-rimmed eyes in the front room of the house, doing nothing. She went to her brother, who had been living in the neighborhood for the last few years, for advice. He told her that Demitrios was a loafer; the trouble with him was that he had never been properly disciplined. Marika's sister, Anna, who had married a Greek wrestler and also settled in Lourenço Marques, said the exact opposite. They should let the youngster alone.

In his own haphazard fashion Demitrios explored the various quarters of Lourenço Marques, the docks, the outlying slums to the north. He liked to visit Gregoris, who supplied the whole town with ice cream. The cold storage abutted a house with many rooms. In one of them he got to know Cora, a woman who wore nail polish of a different color every time he visited her; she was Portuguese or possibly colored. He also liked to hang about at the Acropolis, the large, modern department store in the center of town, where everything was for sale and spread out for inspection. In the evenings he went to the Contes' gym, where they called him "Skinny." He boxed featherweight, flailing his arms wildly in the ring. No one took him seriously as a contender. He didn't have it in him.

One afternoon he lay in bed with Betty Boop. No one else was at home. The two of them had taken off nearly all their clothes, but it was not clear to him who had taken the initiative. Mimis stroked her shoulder.

After the murder of Verwoerd, Tsafendas was questioned for days at a time by the security police. Several times they went over the story of his life. On Monday morning, 12 September 1966, he said he had forgotten to tell them something important the previous night. What he then declared threw a startlingly different light on the unhappy relations within his family between 1925 and 1927, when he had first been sent away to school—and indeed subsequently. His stepmother, he said, had abused him. Because he was heir to his father's property, Marika had turned the whole family against him. She was determined to destroy his "masculine qualities." Having used that unusual phrase, Demitrios followed it with another. She began, he said, "to *corrupt* me." He felt that he had been spoiled and defiled. Even before his departure for Middelburg she had persuaded her brother to rape him.

"My uncle dragged me into a room and committed an unnatural deed with me. I got very scared. I was just a child."

It sounded as if he had plucked the story out of thin air. It appeared to have been put together out of tales from the experiences of others or from events that had happened earlier or later in his life. Demitrios looked at his past as if through a kaleidoscope—depending on need or desire, he would give it a quarter turn this way or that.

He regarded the period between 1934 and 1935, after he left the school in Middelburg and was living again in Lourenço Marques, as the most painful he ever went through. In retrospect he felt it was then that he had been most vulnerable to what he called "corruption." It was then, he insisted, that his view of himself and of the world at large had darkened and hardened irrevocably.

Of the hiding given to him by his father when he came home and found Mimis and Betty Boop in bed together, Demitrios could remember little, except that he had lost consciousness or, rather, that he had come around while the Portuguese doctor was attending to him. His aunt Anna was trying to calm Marika. For many days afterward she would not address a single word to him. During this time Michaelis simply stayed away from the house. Demitrios could not understand why his father had attacked him so violently. Evangelina and he often lay on top of each other, in the garden, too—tickling each other, playing leapfrog, carrying on like crazy people. Sometimes they pretended that her bed was a boat. Betty Boop was by far his best friend in the family.

He was kept out of school, not as a punishment but because after that episode he began to be overcome by attacks of uncontrollable rage. His parents were afraid of what he might do to the other pupils. He refused to eat for a week and they could do nothing but call the doctor again to come and see him. He was left with a bottle of tonic of which he was to drink a tablespoon a day until he felt better. The doctor recommended exposure to sunlight, too. Every day he was to spend such and such a period in the sun. After a month of this treatment he was almost as dark as an African. He refused to go back to the mission school, even when he himself declared that he now felt much better. Finally they arrived at a compromise. Mimis would go to evening classes at an English-language institution in the town.

Michaelis Tsafandakis eventually came to the decision that he no longer had a future in Mozambique. The family should move to Pretoria as soon as possible. He would go ahead, to find a job and a place for the family to live in. Marika would follow with the children. And Demitrios? The ambitions that Michaelis had once nurtured for him were by now much moderated; his erratic behavior ruled them out. It was clear that he would never become an engineer of any kind, like his father. Given the state of race relations in South Africa it would probably be better for him to remain in Lourenço Marques. Talking to the Greek owner of the Acropolis, Mr. Sideris, Michaelis suggested that a place might be found for the boy in the store—possibly in the kiosk selling books and magazines.

Mimis saw little of his father in the months before the family's departure. Nothing Michaelis said to him assuaged his conviction that he was being abandoned. Even his stepmother suddenly seemed to be more concerned about how he would manage in the future than Michaelis, the man who had previously been the most important figure in his life.

In the late summer of 1935 Marika saw to it that a medicine against tapeworms, prescribed by the Portuguese doctor Mimis had been seeing, was administered to him. On one of the succeeding days, to Marika's surprise and relief, a worm two or three feet long was found in his stool. That was the explanation, presumably, of his underfed appearance.

Mimis wanted to take the entire stool to the doctor to investigate. Had the doctor not promised he would? Mimis also wanted to be certain that the head of the creature did not remain in his bowels. But ignoring his protests, Marika washed the entire mess down the toilet. Too late, she realized how much importance he had attached to it. On hearing what she had done he rushed into the kitchen and began hammering on the cupboard with his fist—hammering and hammering. When he paused for a moment Marika gave him money and told him to buy an ice cream with it. He turned around and threw the coins out the window. What did she think he was—a child?

Mimis felt as if a door had been slammed shut. Left behind in Lourenço Marques, he no longer had any obligations to the family and could do whatever he wished. He regarded Marika's assurance that he would always be welcome in Pretoria as pure hypocrisy. They were glad to be rid of him. Nonetheless, in August 1935 he asked for permission from the South African Interior Ministry to enter the country to visit his family. The application was a formality, he thought. Five months later he received a note telling him that his application had been refused.

Mimis was bitterly disappointed—and suspicious. The South African consulate in Lourenço Marques would not elaborate. And suddenly the local Greek community held him in disregard. His stepuncle, Marika's brother, would have nothing to do with him. In any case, this uncle was about to leave for Rhodesia, where he planned to become a tobacco farmer. Mr. Sideris, for whom Mimis now sorted newspapers, arranged the books in the kiosk, and helped with the cash sales, allowed him to take back to his little apartment each day a free copy of the *Lourenço Marques Guardian*. But it was clear that Mrs. Sideris did not want him to come near her house. Was she afraid for her daughters? He was now seventeen years old, a head taller than her husband, taller than his own father.

Mimis could not let the matter rest. The Sideris girls were as pretty as pictures. With their pale oval faces and black hair they reminded him—or so he liked to believe—of the girls of Alexandria.

When he made an unannounced visit to the Sideris house and, omitting the usual greetings in Greek, went straight to the gramophone, Mrs. Sideris shouted at him abruptly.

"You're just like your mother," she said.

He looked at her in astonishment.

"Your mother, your real mother, was a black, a colored woman. A mulatto," she repeated, in Portuguese.

He heard her, but he regarded what she had said as just another of the many obscure insults and accusations he had shaken off before. He was a Greek, the son of a Greek, the grandson of a Greek. He left the house without replying. The following day, however, he went to the office of the Administraçao Civil. He looked up the records there, and for the first time in his life read the name of his mother: Amelia Williams. She had died nine years earlier, in one of the "native" areas of Lourenço Marques—on 12 January 1927, two days before his ninth birthday. Someone in the office confirmed for him that she was a colored, of part-Swazi origins.

Suddenly he had to think of himself in two parts, as a kind of double: one half this, the other that; half *nonwhite,* the other half . . . acceptable. In South Africa *White* and *Swazi* were written with capital letters, as if they referred to nations; *mulatto* and *bastard,* with lowercase letters, for such people were without consequence—they had come from nowhere and would amount to nothing. He listened to the fan going around and around just below the ceiling of his room. Who, then, were his grandparents?

He returned to the Administraçao Civil and went from office to office seeking information that might be relevant to him, but he came out with nothing. One file said that Amelia Williams had a German father, another that her father was English. No one could tell him where she was buried.

For Tsafendas, now eighteen years old, everything he had always felt to be suspect or ominous about himself fell into place. His tightly curled hair. His skin color—which he had thought of as Mediterranean. Grandmother Tsafendas's vagueness whenever he asked about his mother. The resentment and hostility of Marika and the contempt his uncle showed him. The teasing at school. The negative reply from the South African immigration service. The tentative, curious glances constantly thrown at him; the indefinable hesitation with which people greeted him.

In one blow he had become other to himself, irrevocably. He now knew himself to be literally and figuratively the black sheep of the family. And the authorities in the neighboring country, South Africa, knew all about him too.

He did not, however, abandon his hopes of joining his family there. By this time Michaelis was working as a welder for the state-owned Iron and Steel Corporation (ISCOR). Again Mimis applied for permission to enter the country; again the consulate in Lourenço Marques reported that it would not be granted.

He consoled himself as best he could with Cora, the woman with painted nails who lived in the house of many rooms.

Of all foods, Demitrios most loved lobster. He told me so, with much emphasis, when I visited him for the first time in the psychiatric institution in the Transvaal in which he had long been incarcerated. The giant crabs that his stepmother had served up in Lourenço Marques were splendid too. But nothing could beat lobster or langoustine.

"The best food I ever ate, lobster."

The ward attendant, a hefty man in a white coat who happened to be passing at that moment, turned to us with a grimace. "Lobster? What's lobster?" he asked, but before we could answer he let the door to the kitchen bang shut behind him.

People in the interior of the country are often suspicious of seafood. Creatures that live in their shells are thought to be disgusting, impure somehow.

As a schoolboy Demitrios had made the journey between Mozambique and the Transvaal at least a dozen times, traveling uncomfortably on the steam train that connected the Indian Ocean coastline with the great plateau two thousand meters higher that is the heartland of South Africa. In 1936 he decided to follow his family to Pretoria, despite the authorities' refusal to give him a visa to enter the country. He knew just how porous, how poorly controlled, the borders were. That fall he concealed himself among some machinery packed in a cargo car and crossed the border at Komatipoort with no difficulty. Then on to Pretoria.

For some time after his arrival he worked in the Fountains Cafe, not far from the railway station. He scrubbed tables and ran about the streets on errands, often with a tray in his hand. For the first but not for the last time in his career he was living as an illegal immigrant, someone who had slipped through officaldom's nets. On the Witwatersrand—the sprawling metropolis of Johannesburg and its surroundings—there were many thousands of others in the same position. The depression of the previous few years had coincided with a severe drought on the highveld. Needy farmers, both white and black, as well as poverty-stricken families from the neighboring Portuguese and British colonies, streamed toward the city. Most of them would never return to the rural areas from which they had come. The struggle for existence among these newcomers was inevitably fought along racial lines and hence on unequal terms. The whites had the vote, and their representatives in parliament passed law after law to protect their constituents against competition from the blacks.

Demitrios had not been warmly received by his family in Pretoria. His brother, Victor, had come to regard himself as the oldest son and Marika encouraged him to do so. Contact between Demitrios and the others was seldom pleasant. Within two months he had moved to Hillbrow, a suburb of Johannesburg not far from the center of the city. There he went from one menial job to another, usually in the restaurant business. From the City Tearoom to the Elgin Cafe in Jeppe Street and from there to the Cosmopolitan Restaurant.

He was almost nineteen years old. His employers found him friendly enough though also touchy sometimes. Those who got to know him better thought him talkative, intelligent, given to daydreaming. While on his own in Lourenço Marques he had changed, turned a corner. The introverted, hollow-chested pubescent had become a rough, loquacious young man who was proud of the languages he knew and of the ideas he could express in all of them. He read the newspapers and kept abreast of political issues: the strikes in the gold mines, the behavior of the police—who would go hunting the streets for blacks without passes—and the agitation to revise the electoral laws and strike off the rolls that tiny minority of "non-Europeans"—1 percent of the electorate—who still retained the right to vote.

Spokesmen for the government of General Jan Smuts and J. B. M. Hertzog declared that a shared vote would lead directly to shared beds and bastardization.

Demitrios allowed himself to be taken by some acquaintances to meetings of the Communist Party, a noisy but ineffective little groupuscule. Films from the Soviet Union were shown in one of the city's cinemas. Small private gatherings were also addressed by the party's intellectuals. What he saw and heard during these meetings he guilelessly tried to pass on to the clients of the restaurants he worked in. Perhaps more provocatively still, he occasionally distributed pamphlets on behalf of the party.

It is not known who finally gave his name to police headquarters in Marshall Square. Perhaps he had unwisely drawn attention to himself by trying to get his situation in the country regularized. In the winter he was picked up and deported to Mozambique.

From then on he was kept under surveillance by the authorities in both Mozambique and the Union of South Africa. Nor was the stigma of his mother's origins forgotten. Besides, he was incapable of holding his tongue. In Lourenço Marques he attempted to enlist in the Portuguese army, but on principle the recruiting office turned away people of mixed racial origin. He went back to his old job selling books and periodicals in the Acropolis department store. Within a few weeks his incessant carrying on had turned his colleagues against him. He was put out on the street.

A time of great anxiety followed. His deportation from South Africa had reawakened old insecurities. He slept badly. He suffered from severe indigestion. In the early mornings he would wake to a turbulence in his stomach.

He lived in hand-to-mouth fashion, sometimes working as a porter on the docks, sometimes hanging around the Catholic mission or the Anglican church, where many members of the Greek community used to attend services. He relaxed in the company of blacks, among whom he could even play the hero or the boss, like his father. But the more he felt himself going downhill socially, the less he could understand or control what he was becoming.

To his surprise he was given a job, in the winter of 1937, by the British state airline, Imperial Airways. A new airport was being built in the most northerly province of Mozambique, on the marshy, malarial coast near Quelimane, and the firm needed a translator who knew Portuguese and Shangaan—though he had to struggle to master the latter language. Out in the swamps and bushveld no one cared what exactly his status or his parentage was. He could make his own way there. He learned to drive a car and chauffeured his superiors around.

His leisure hours he spent studying the few technical books he could get hold of in that isolated corner of the world. Sometimes he browsed in an English translation of the Bible that the previous occupant of his quarters had left behind. During this period he made friends with a mechanical engineer from Scotland who went by the name of Scotty. The man was a rough, extroverted type who was not much interested in Mimis's tales. He organized hunting parties that went out into the marshes not far from the mouth of the Zambesi. Plenty of game was to be found there. The employees of Imperial Airways earned pocket money by exporting buffalo meat to Rhodesia and Nyasaland.

Scotty lived with a black woman from a neighboring tribe.

"How can you go with someone like that?" Mimis once asked.

She was terrific in bed, Scotty answered. He laughed loudly. "She can take the skin off your dick."

Mimis thought to himself: Never mind.

Alone at night in his little room, he would fantasize about his fate. His real mother must have been an exceptional woman. Just as black and no less fierce than Scotty's friend. What had actually happened between her and Michaelis? Could it be that she had brought into being some kind of new, separate tribe? Where that particular idea had come from he did not know. Perhaps she had not died but had left his father for her own reasons and somewhere, in a secret corner of Africa, was ruling over a group of rebellious women of mixed race. Sometimes these thoughts took forms more grotesque still. His own imaginings pursued him. They were out of control.

"Out of control," he said to Scotty matter-of-factly. The words remained without concrete meaning, like the clouds moving above the head of the surprised Scotsman, traveling toward the tangled, indolent bush and then vanishing.

Overcome by severe stomach pains, Demitrios was admitted to the nearest clinic, where his appendix was removed by a local doctor. The anesthetic seemed to remain in his system and continued to affect his daydreams for weeks afterward. He fell silent; stood motionless for minutes on end, unable to utter a sound; moved tentatively, like a partially blind person. The operation seemed to him to have cut him off from his own being. His body had become what the locals called *dungeka:* husklike, set apart.

Scotty could no longer understand him and Demitrios could not explain how he felt. In the evening, as he was about to enter his cabin, he would hear through the half-open door the cry of a muezzin becoming one with a sound that came from the stars. At other times he heard the hiss of a snake. He would find himself in an underground vault and would be compelled to listen to the snake. It made a horrible, urgent, incomprehensible sound.

These anxiety attacks went on for three or four weeks. He was barely able to keep himself going. Such things were not uncommon in Quelimane, among either the half-crazy expatriates or the mocking, malignant natives. After about a month the feeling that he was under constant threat began to recede slowly. Mimis was able at last to think about other things. Like travel. Air travel especially. Though he had yet to set foot in an airplane, the idea of doing so roused his enthusiasm.

In January 1938, his Quelimane experience now well behind him, Demitrios went to the South African consulate in Lourenço Marques and made yet another request for permission to live in the country. On this occasion he made sure that the translation of the Portuguese birth certificate presented to the consul showed Marika (who was registered as white in the records) and not Amelia Williams as his natural mother. This maneuver did not help. In July he applied to the consulate simply for a tourist visa. That, too, was denied him. He was not welcome in South Africa, not even as a tourist. He managed to slip into the country again nevertheless.

He was determined that this time no one would know where he was going or what he was doing.

Then silence. More than a year passed before his name resurfaced in the official South African files. This time it was because he had meticulously gone to register himself at police headquarters in Marshall Square, Johannesburg. For the next three months he attended Progress College in that city. He studied electrical welding, metal cutting with an oxyacetylene burner, and lathe work. The moment he received his certificate from the college he signed on as a member of a trade union, the Boiler Makers and Welders Union.

These were feverish times. The South African economy was expanding rapidly; the Second World War was about to break out and skilled labor was in short supply. At the beginning of May 1939, Demitrios found work with the British Mining Supply Company on Faraday Street. The firm had recently switched to the production of armored vehicles; his speciality was producing filters and pump cowlings.

Demitrios invested in a tailor-made suit and crocodile shoes. His work turned out to be not too arduous. Whenever he did not want to work or felt too weak, he stayed in bed. No one was going to make a fuss about it. He soon got in touch with the Communists again. He paid his monthly subscription of two shillings and sixpence to the party and went up and down Loveday Street distributing leaflets. Every now and then he attended meetings on the City Hall steps or in various community centers. What he most enjoyed, however, were his visits to the local library. He spent hours there, bent over the latest technical and scientific journals. He was now interested in technology, maritime architecture, astronomy, and metallurgy.

These journals made him long for "overseas," the lands where everything was more modern, moved more rapidly, and was less provincial than in South Africa. Would it not be a great thing to stand one day in London's famous Trafalgar Square? Or among the skyscrapers of New York?

Twenty months after Demitrios formally registered his presence in the country, some anonymous official in some department or other scrutinized the Tsafendas dossier and found that not everything was as it should be. Demitrios had committed an offense under the Aliens Act, which governed all aspects of immigration. On 6 August 1940 he was summoned to appear before a judge. He was found guilty of contravening the act and sentenced either to pay a fine of twelve pounds and ten shillings or to spend a month in prison. Demitrios was relieved at the outcome. His employers, British Mining, had presented to the court a statement from which nothing suspicious or untoward about him could be elicited, and it had been decided not to expel him from the country. He paid the fine immediately and temporary papers were issued to him, on the grounds of his claim that he was performing "essential war service."

But another zealous pen pusher in the Department of

Immigration and Asiatic Affairs was not satisfied. He wanted to know why the case of Tsafendas had been dealt with so leniently. This official's department head was persuaded to send a note to the commissioner of police informing him of the following damaging facts: the man was a half-caste—a colored—and a Communist. Further: "The above is passed to you in order that the activities of Tsafandakis [*sic*] may be watched, and I shall be glad if you will advise me in due course should anything to his detriment become known."

Was this the reason that six months later Demitrios left his "war job" with the British Mining Supply Company? At the beginning of 1942 he applied at the consulate in Johannesburg for a Portuguese passport. The document issued to him was valid for one year only. The Greek consulate, to which he had also applied for a passport, issued him a document that, like the other, was valid for just a year. He knew that he would not be left to himself for much longer; the security services were watching his comings and goings. In May he left for Cape Town. His intention was to sign on with a ship sailing for Great Britain or the United States. The Greek consul in Cape Town helped him get a job on the cargo ship *Eugenie Livanos*. Its destination was the east coast of Canada.

On the day of his departure Mimis climbed Table Mountain. The view over South Africa's mother city and the bay was spectacular. To the left were the white crests of the Atlantic Ocean. To the right, in the distance, he could see the mother-of-pearl peaks of the Hottentot's Holland mountains. The wind hissed among the rocks and slopes around him; the noise of the city below was barely audible. It was as if he saw it all through a tinted wall of glass.

Jumbled thoughts passed through his mind. He was leaving the region of his birth to prove that he was a man at home in the wide world, that he was no bastard but a cosmopolitan. He broke off the tapering silver leaf of a shrub he could not name and put it inside his Bible. Then he wandered slowly down to the docks.

It is hard for us today to imagine the expectations that Cape Town harbor once aroused in those who passed through it, whether arriving at the quasi-mythical foot of Africa or departing from it certain of one thing only: the difficulty, perhaps the impossibility, of ever returning. The emptiness between departure and landfall, the void the ocean used to represent to those crossing it, the tedium and formlessness that provoked a longing for the shore, any shore—all that has been lost. The difference between the Cape and the "real world" once amounted to seven thousand nautical miles; at sea it was experienced as an interminable period of suspension, a yawning hiatus in the lives of everyone on board.

On 12 June 1942 Demitrios Tsafendas sailed northward, not knowing that twenty years would pass before he returned to the city.

Twenty-four-year-old Demitrios did not think of the crew of the *Eugenie Livanos* as a group of strangers. They were Greeks; they spoke his father's language; he felt he knew their ways. But after a while he took a dislike to the hothouse atmosphere of the ship, the dependence of the sailors on one another, the isolated, hierarchical nature of their closely knit society. In it he occupied the lowliest rank of all. He had the title of mess boy and served the others: kneading dough in the kitchen, pulling loaves out of the oven. At first he was teased, sent about the ship on long, pointless errands. When he complained to the officers they shrugged their shoulders and laughed.

Demitrios was on board because he wanted to get out of South Africa. Now he found himself among rejects—flamboyant, dope-smoking, foul-mouthed types who brandished knives. The ship was ruled by the ethos of "setting the guts on fire," as the Greek song put it, the ethos of the rover's existence that rotted one's insides. And it was wartime. The farther north the ship sailed the more Demitrios's unease grew. Panic overtook him when he realized that his flight might be doomed from the outset. Once they had crossed the equator and the *Eugenie Livanos* entered the war zone of the North Atlantic, where German U-boats roamed, Demitrios withdrew into himself and fell sick. He pined for land long before the ship finally entered Canadian waters.

No sooner had they berthed in St. John's harbor than he packed his few things and fled.

It was autumn in America. Demitrios was picked up by the police near Montreal. He begged the Canadian authorities not to send him back to the *Livanos*. He spent months under informal arrest in Halifax, Nova Scotia. The Canadians were not sure what to do with him.

In the winter of 1942 he escaped, together with two other

sailors who had jumped ship. After a journey of five hundred kilometers they reached the border of the United States. On foot and in daunting conditions, Demitrios crossed the frozen St. Croix River. Three weeks later he was picked up in Bangor, Maine, and arrested for entering the United States illegally. On his arrest he started babbling nonsense, gibberish; with some deliberateness, in all likelihood, he presented himself to his captors as a man who was deeply disturbed. These were the circumstances of his first admission to a psychiatric institution. It was attached to a hospital in Boston. He did his best there to convince the doctors that he heard voices, that horrible voices spoke to him out of the hospital's central heating system. After a while he no longer needed to exaggerate the state he was in; it seemed that the long ocean voyage had indeed unhinged him.

Any hope of getting permission to reside in the United States, which had been his original aim, was now ruled out. Demitrios's next four years were spent either in detention or in service on the so-called Liberty Ships—cheaply and hastily built freighters that sailed the Atlantic in convoys to supply the Allies with food and arms. He was hospitalized six times altogether in different institutions during this period, sometimes in a serious condition, sometimes with complaints that appear to have been trifling. Each time he was discharged he was sent straight back to sea. When he was not in the hospital he was on board ship—always against his will.

The spring of 1945 found him on another Greek vessel, the *Marina Nicolao*. From there he wrote a letter to President

Roosevelt complaining that over the last few years he had spent no more than twenty-nine days ashore and at liberty. Now that Nazi Germany was on the point of capitulating, could his "war service" be taken into account and permission for him to reside legally in the United States finally be granted?

From March 1946 on he spent eighteen months on land, in North Grafton State Hospital in Massachusetts. The prognosis, according to the doctors, was poor. Demitrios hallucinated; he spoke of a girl who was waiting for him somewhere in southern Africa, but at the same time he expressed his conviction that all his progeny would be black. In January 1947 his condition was described as "hebephrenic schizophrenia," a form of schizophrenia that sets in at an early age. Six months later he was declared cured and discharged. The doctors wanted him to be repatriated, and in the meantime details of his previous life had filtered through to the authorities. The fact that he had been a member of the Communist Party was regarded as even more sinister in postwar America than it had been in the Transvaal some years earlier.

The officials who scratched their heads over Demitrios's future had to determine who he was and to what country he belonged. There was no simple answer to either question, for the officials were dealing with someone who had as many identities as moods.

Was he the illegitimate son of a lathe operator now living in Pretoria? A Mozambican agitator? A South African *métique* of Greek background? A deranged sailor? Apart from fluent

Greek, English, and Portuguese, he spoke Shangaan, Arabic, and a little Afrikaans. His Greek and Portuguese passports had long since expired. He possessed the papers of an American seaman, but these were of doubtful value. South Africa offered no solution to the problem, only a clear indication that he would not be welcome there. The authorities confirmed that they had refused him a visa several times already and would refuse again if he should seek one.

Somewhere in those offices, with the Bakelite telephones and packed filing cabinets, the knot was finally severed. Demitrios Tsafandakis, it was declared, was *definitely* Greek.

In August a deportation order was issued. A month later, under police escort, he was put aboard the SS *Marine Jumbo*. The ship was about to sail to the Mediterranean, calling at Piraeus, the port for the city of Athens.

Piraeus in the sunset light of 1947. The harbor a random assemblage of fortified, bomb-battered structures. Hawkers and peddlers swarming on the sidewalks. The cafés filled with men, men only, most of them moustached and unemployed. The daily papers under strict censorship. Streets reeking of gasoline and sesame. Turkish hookahs for hire. On every corner rousing gramophone music of the kind Demitrios remembered from his parents' house in Lourenço Marques. He was at last free, ashore legally, done with the fear of being followed.

Not that all was well. A civil war was in progress. German occupation and years of starvation had been succeeded by guerrilla fighting; now an outright war was being fought between the left and the right. Demitrios had arrived in a country with an empty stomach and darkness in its heart. Yet he was about to enjoy a period that was free of the attacks that had been tormenting him since he left Cape Town. It was as if here, precisely here, he had at last acquired some of the stoic fatalism that the Greeks think of as peculiarly their own. Like many another macho Greek, he also learned to boast and complain. He talked himself into a job with the American Mission for Aid to Greece, a subsection of the Marshall Plan. He worked first as a translator, subsequently in the branch dealing with the delivery of supplies to American and British troops. He had status again, he used his languages, he bought a hat.

Nevertheless, he applied more than once for a visa to reside in South Africa or at least to visit the country, and in the letters accompanying these applications he did his best to deny that he actually "belonged" in Europe. A hectoring tone began to enter into his correspondence with both the South African Department of External Affairs and the American authorities: "I was sent to Greece, a country I have never seen before. . . . It is not a small mistake. The difference is between the North Pole and the South Pole." He insisted that South Africa was the country in which he had been educated and that it was "the country of my mother, Amelia Williams." Just as he had done previously in the United States, he told the story of the woman who had remained faithful to him for so long. "Will you please permit me to go home again and to return to the girl with whom I grew up, whom I want to marry, and with whom I have so much in common." And in conclusion: "I am here a man without a country. . . . I have a lot more to mention but cannot put it into writing."

This letter ends with the words "Remain Yours, James Demitrios Tsafandakis."

He had acquired the name James in Piraeus. In all likelihood this was the consequence of his having joined a group of young men and women who kept in touch with what they called, simply enough, the Christian Church. They met occasionally in one of the suburbs of Athens to study the Scriptures; their chief language was English. The group was not exactly a church, nor was it a sect or cult. Rather, it was a vague, pleasant fellowship of faith with worldwide contacts. Its doctrines, so far as there were any, emphasized the equality of all races, a not very strictly observed abstinence from alcohol, and a peace-loving, almost American kind of optimism. Demitrios's conversion to the faith had been confirmed by baptism in the sea and by his new name. Recently dismissed from the American Mission for Aid, the thirty-year-old but already corpulent James, wearing only his underpants, had been ritually immersed in the waves near Piraeus. After the ceremony he was joyfully applauded and thrown onto the sandy beach.

Demitrios lived in Greece for almost two years—that is, for about as long a period as he had spent on the Witwatersrand. The restlessness and chronic anxiety struck at him again. In the late summer of 1949, he worked for a time on a Greek cruise ship, the *Corinthia,* which went from port to port around the Mediterranean. In Marseilles he left the ship and traveled to Paris, where he applied for a visa to Spain. On 8 November he arrived at a Portuguese border post, Barca d'Alva, only to be arrested by the guards on duty.

He spent a month under arrest in Oporto, while the Policia Internaçional e de Defesa do Estado (President António de Oliveira Salazar's notorious secret police) examined his baptismal certificate. The refugee passport given him in Athens revealed that he had been deported several times from the United States. His putative Portuguese citizenship was investigated and confirmed from Lourenço Marques. But in that case why had he never been called up for military service? Immediately he was declared to be a deserter and locked up. Three months later he appeared before a military tribunal in Lisbon. The PIDE reported that the Mozambique administrators had described him as an unwanted person of alien descent who would not be permitted to reenter the province. The PIDE report also acknowledged, however, that he was not wholly accountable for his actions. He was a vagrant *que tem una vida sempre instável e de aventuras*—"constantly drawn to an unstable and adventurous way of life."

The vagrant was set free, given temporary papers, and allowed to remain in Portugal.

From there he wrote letters to his family in Pretoria. They did not respond. They had no intention of helping him; such feelings of affection as they might once have had were now dead.

For the next year or so he could be seen wandering about the banks of the Tagus, earning his keep by hawking assorted goods of the cheapest kind: little combs, sunglasses, plastic whirligigs. He liked to go aboard ships in the harbor and gossip with their crews. He also made himself as agreeable as he could around the offices of the Companhia Naçional de Navigaçâo. Through his connections there he eventually succeeded in getting a job at sea once more. Destination: Mozambique.

October 1951. The cargo vessel SS *Save* makes it way through the Straits of Gibraltar, sails east, and passes along the Suez Canal. Within a couple of weeks the coasts of East Africa have been left behind. Now it enters Delagoa Bay and is moored in the harbor of Lourenço Marques. Demitrios leans over the railing. What he sees is too beautiful to be believed: the busy quay and, beyond the warehouses, the city of his birth.

Once ashore, however, he is held by passport control. "Dimitrie Tsafandakis" is known to them as a Communist, a draft dodger, a troublemaker. His papers may be in order but he is not allowed to proceed further. He puts up a protest against this treatment, before returning unwillingly to his ship. At noon he reports to its sick bay, doubled over with stomach pains, barely able to stay on his feet. He appears to be suffering from an acute attack of appendicitis. A decision is taken to admit him urgently to a hospital in the city.

No sooner is he off the ship than his condition improves remarkably. He has no time to lose. An hour or two later, he sneaks out of the hospital and makes his way to the honorary Greek consul. He needs a Greek passport to enable him to

travel from Lourenço Marques to Pretoria. Surely that is little
to ask.

The consul for Greece was Tony Maw—that same Tony
Maw who had been a neighbor of Michaelis Tsafandakis
many years before, in the Rua Andrade Corvo. He remembered Mimis both as the little half-breed who had been sent
to his grandmother in Alexandria and as a schoolboy. Now he
was back in his office, after all this time, not lost forever in the
wilderness of the world: a strong, sun-tanned, loutish fellow,
beefy but well-spoken, complaining about his treatment at
the hands of the Portuguese.

For his part, Demitrios was confident that he had come to
the right place. He was dealing with a friend of his father's,
after all. He hadn't seen his family for ten years, he said; he
had been blocked and frustrated everywhere, especially by
the PIDE and the South Africans. It was more than time that
he visited Michaelis, who was now sixty-six years old and was
waiting impatiently to see his long-lost firstborn son.

Maw was not inclined to oblige this interloper by issuing
him a travel document, though doing so would have been no
trouble. Demitrios had arrived in the office out of the blue.
He was not even a Greek citizen, formally speaking. His
father was indeed known to Maw, but it now transpired that
Tsafandakis had never taken the trouble to register the birth
of his illegitimate child with the consulate. Let him plead as
much as he liked; the consul was determined to stick to the
letter of the law. All else aside, Demitrios had feigned illness
in order to get ashore. He was an illegal immigrant. What

could he have been thinking of? Nothing could be simpler, the Englishman said threateningly, than for him to phone the police. Demitrios would be deported immediately.

"Do you know anything about my natural mother?" Demitrios asked, more in an attempt to distract Maw than in hope of rousing his compassion. "I spent years looking for her grave. To tell the truth, I'm not even sure she is actually dead."

The consul was not impressed. He had never known Amelia, he said curtly. According to reports, she was not someone who was fit to be a life's companion for the good-hearted Michaelis. She was black, a "native."

Hesitantly, Demitrios took his hat off. His legs began to tremble. He did not know what to say. A few minutes later Maw told the eccentric seaman to leave.

"Just remember that one day I won't want a Greek Ortho-dox funeral," Demitrios shouted weakly, from outside the office.

Not long after this episode the authorities returned him to Lisbon. He was trapped like an eel in a basket, it seemed, and would never escape. His old ailments duly reappeared. In the Hospital do Ultramar a diagnosis was made: "parasitose intes-tinal; psicose maníaco-depressiva." On this occasion, how-ever, the parasites in his intestines and brain apparently responded rapidly to treatment, for he was discharged from the hospital after a mere three weeks.

The PIDE was convinced that he was up to no good. He was arrested trying to cross the border into Spain; for this he spent the next eleven months in jail. Initially he was kept in the "Aljube," where political prisoners were interrogated; later he was put in one of the cells in Fort Calxias. In both places he was manhandled as never before. Nothing in his previous experience had prepared him for such treatment. A couple of times he feared for his life; in the Portugal of the dictator Salazar anything was possible. But the interrogations yielded nothing and toward the end of April 1953 he was set free.

He found himself in the Albergue de Mendicida de Mitra, a shelter for the homeless run by an order of mendicant friars in Lisbon. He became a peddler once again. Along the quays and avenues of the capital he carried his wares: lacework, this time, and local embroidery, along with various gewgaws.

The extent and complexity of Tsafendas's wanderings stun the imagination. But it is possible to discern one common theme. During the two decades he spent outside South Africa the sea was the only constant presence in his life. He remained almost exclusively on the coastlines of the countries in which he lived, in cities where the docks beckoned him and where the sounds of winches, seagulls, and motors rose above the hiss and roar of the ocean. Piraeus, Oporto, Lisbon, Marseilles, London, Hamburg—he was most himself amid the restless, provisional lives of people who did not know where they might be the next day or the day after. It was as if unspoken judgment had been passed on him: once he had reached a certain age and had gone a certain distance, he was compelled to serve out his days within earshot of the clamor of waves and spray.

In all likelihood Demitrios would never have managed to get back to South Africa had it not been for the profound unpredictability of circumstance inherent to his way of life. In the 1950s and early 1960s, it seemed he would not succeed in returning to the subcontinent. One wonders why he longed to return there, where he would be more conspicuous than anywhere else and, above all, where he would be regarded as a half-man, a member of a subspecies. From 1951 on, his name appears on the official list of those banned from entering South Africa—the so-called blacklist. In Portugal the PIDE would always be suspicious of him. He had been permanently excluded from the United States. A period in Germany had ended in the Ochsenzoll Clinic; after his discharge he was dispatched to Lisbon, where he again plied his trade as a hawker along the Tagus and in the city's parks. Some two years later he attended the Brussels trade fair, optimistically bringing with him a stock of Portuguese embroidery. For the failure of this particular venture he later blamed "the Chinese competition." In the spring of 1959, after a further spell in Germany, Demitrios decided (in his words) "to leave western Europe and try my luck in England."

The move did nothing to improve his circumstances. As a foreigner, the holder of a Portuguese passport, he was denied an official work permit. Casual jobs were hard to come by, and he found the place and the people unfriendly. Nevertheless, he managed to keep himself going until fall. Always a lover of public debate, he was fascinated by Speakers' Corner in Hyde Park and went to meetings of the Labor Party at Caxton Hall, where he heard speeches by Barbara Castle and the future prime minister, James Callaghan. He also attended gatherings of the nascent anti-apartheid movement and, more unexpectedly, established contact with a self-styled neo-Labor group that used the North Middlesex Cricket Club—of all improbable venues—as its meeting place. There were a number of disaffected anti-apartheid ex–South Africans in this group, one of whom remembered "Tsafandakis" explicitly introducing himself to them as a Cape Colored. He was eager, Demitrios said, "to create resistance to the regime," though he had no plausible suggestions as to how this might be done. While in London he made a further attempt to gain entry papers for South Africa; that approach, like all those that had preceded it, was firmly rebuffed by the authorities.

Early in his stay in London, Demitrios was admitted for examination to both University College Hospital and the Hospital for Tropical Diseases; each time he came in complaining of stomach disorders. Predictably enough, the doctors were unable to help him. He did not blame them for their failure; to him it was evidence of how difficult and special his case was. Later his condition deteriorated radically. In mid-September he was admitted to St. Pancras Hospital in a psychotic state. The episode was brief, but it was followed by a more protracted collapse, which led to two months' confinement in Whitecroft Hospital on the Isle of Wight. On his release the authorities gave him a choice: he could be sent back either to Germany or to Portugal. Staying on in the United Kingdom was out of the question. Demitrios chose

Germany. From there he made yet another attempt to reach southern Africa.

Overland, this time.

On 30 June 1960 Demitrios left by train from Munich for the Balkans. After a short stop in Piraeus he traveled to Alexandria, the city of his childhood. Arriving there in October, he was arrested almost immediately. Toward the end of that year he was helped by the Red Cross to get passage on a boat going to Beirut. Some weeks later his presence in East Jerusalem was noted. He made an effort to enter Israel, carrying a small suitcase in each hand. Absolutely penniless, he could not convince the officials at the Mandelbaum Gate of his good intentions. "Is there no place here for a mendicant monk?" he demanded of them. An investigator was summoned and after a short conversation he was sent back to the Jordanian sector of the city. A note was taken of the interview, and thus Tsafendas's name was entered into the dossiers of the Mossad, too.

For months Mimis went back and forth across the two sides of the Jordan River. The little Arabic he spoke, far from helping him, was a source of unease to the people he encountered and on at least one occasion led to an ugly misunderstanding and a broken nose. This was when he had to be treated by a Jerusalem doctor—Dr. Theodore Phylactopoulos. Claiming to be a political refugee, he also visited the Spanish embassy in East Jerusalem. But the Spaniards were not prepared to help him get a visa to Israel. Finally he left Jordan on a bus bound for Beirut via Damascus.

He was unable to find work in Lebanon. He set out once more by bus, this time heading toward Tripoli and subsequently to Aleppo, in Syria. From Aleppo it was possible to reach Adana, in Turkey. A difficult trek through the snow-covered passes of the Taurus Mountains brought him to Ankara. Demitrios, the Wandering Greek, had in the meantime grown a beard. His upper jaw was inflamed. His teeth were in a bad state, some of them had crumbled away, and he suffered constantly from pain in his gums.

After a month in Ankara he had picked up some Turkish, a language his father had been able to speak. There were several things here that reminded him of Michaelis: Turkish cuisine, the songs he heard in the teahouses. Even the physical appearance of the men, a certain pride or boldness in their gaze, as well as their habit of sharing the pleasures of a hookah on the sidewalk, seemed reminiscent to him, like a vague echo of the lives of the Cretan forebears he had never known. The same was true of Istanbul. The look of the streets struck him as somehow familiar too, and he himself went about unnoticed through them. With his beard and his belly he could easily be taken for any down-and-out Muslim.

For want of anything better he sold his blood regularly to the Istanbul blood transfusion service. Most of the money he earned in this way—for each pint he was paid about an average week's wage in Turkey—he spent on the dentist. His upper teeth were ground, the incisors filed down, and a gold bridge was fitted. Over it was spread a silver layer. At the age of thirty-five Demitrios had acquired a steely smile.

Later he got a job at Tarhaban College. He taught English and for a while lived with a Turkish woman who also worked at the college. She did what she could for him and, with a word here and a word there, managed to get him a residence permit. In the winter the relationship between them deteriorated; when he left the city—this time for Lisbon via Rome—he carried in his wallet a reference from the college. In it he was referred to as a teacher of English phonetics.

After seaman, translator, lathe operator, hawker, and pilgrim, Demitrios now described himself, when the opportunity arose, as "professor of English."

Then the unexpected happened. For the first time Marika answered one of his letters. A full year after the event he learned that his father had died. Demitrios wrote back to Marika to let her know that although he was still unable to get a visa to enter South Africa he expected to receive his share of the inheritance. By this time he was back in Lisbon. Soon after receiving her letter he went to the South African embassy and applied for a visa. The young woman at the desk told him in a loud voice that the request was pointless. He had been blacklisted by the Ministry of External Affairs and instead of wasting his money trying to get a visa he would do better to spend it on something useful. A clean shirt, for instance. Demitrios flew into a rage. He tore up the application form he had been completing and threw the scraps in her face. Then, still enraged, he left the building.

His next stop was the shelter for the homeless run by the

mendicant friars of Mitra, in which he had taken refuge once before. But he soon got on the wrong side of his benefactors there. They said he made trouble among the other residents. They were tired of listening to his lectures about Palestine, the Bible, and the bad state of affairs in Portugal's colonies. The friars wrote letters to Pretoria: Could the man's family not take care of him? He was lonely and longed for a home. They even got in touch with the PIDE. Why could Demitrios not go back to the country of his birth? He was now forty-five; the whole issue of his conscription had in effect been resolved by the passage of time.

It is hard to know who, if anyone, might have been pulling strings behind the scenes. In August 1963 Demitrios heard that the colonial administration of Mozambique, after thirteen years of hostility, had granted him a sort of amnesty. The brothers of the Albergue de Mendicade de Mitra paid for his passage on a ship called the *Princippi Perfecto*.

Early in October the *Princippi Perfecto* steamed into Delagoa Bay. Once ashore in Lorenço Marques, Demitrios went to stay with his aunt Anna, Marika's sister, who in earlier years had occasionally protected him against the wrath of the family. At Anna's request, Marika arrived from Pretoria a few days later. She told him straight out that Michaelis had left nothing to his oldest son. The family had never been well-off: that was something he must understand once and for all. The small properties Michaelis had owned he had left to his daughters, as their dowry. There had been nothing else.

He was deeply disappointed. Could she, he asked, at least arrange for him to stay for a while under her roof in the Transvaal? Marika phoned her brother in Pretoria. He owned a car. It was agreed that Victor would come get them.

On Saturday morning, 2 November 1963, Demitrios went to the South African consulate in Lourenço Marques and asked for a permit that would allow him a period of temporary residence in the Republic of South Africa. A Mr. J. van der Berg, the official responsible, made a cursory search for the name of Tsafendas on the "Stop List" and failed to find it. As far as J. van der Berg was concerned, the man possessed a valid Portuguese passport, in which he was described as a resident of Mozambique. He was accompanied by members of a family with South African identity papers. Besides, van der Berg was sure that had there been anything suspect about this Tsafendas, he would certainly have heard of it from the PIDE.

On Monday, 4 November, the family—Demitrios, Marika, Victor, and Anna—entered South Africa via the customs post at Komatipoort.

The South Africa that Demitrios was entering was in most respects the same country as the one he had left two decades before—only worse. The Afrikaner Nationalist Party, under Verwoerd, was in the saddle and ruling relentlessly. Segregation was enforced even more strictly than before: laws against marriages and sexual acts between the races were in effect, as were draconian pass laws requiring blacks to carry identity documents at all times ("movement control" was their stated aim). Forcible clearances of black and mixed-race areas in larger and smaller cities took place on a regular basis. After the Sharpeville rebellion of 1960 the prime minister had adumbrated an ideology of so-called separate development, which involved the delineation of bantustans, or "homelands," for blacks. The logic of the program—white tribalism fortified, deepened, aggrandized—astonished even his own supporters. In practice it meant little more than large-scale deportations of blacks to various remote, impoverished corners of the country.

Mimis stepped eagerly into his brother's house. As far as he was concerned he had come home an older and a wiser person. He bought a bicycle.

Why was Demitrios never regarded as a hero by the black population of South Africa? Admittedly, after the assassination in 1966 his name was used by some black youths as a kind of byword. "I'll Tsafendas you" meant "I'll cut you up good." Anyone who could stab a man three or four times in a matter of seconds as virtually every member of parliament looked on had to be thought of as a master craftsman, a specialist. So plainly did this appear to be the case that rumors began to go around that Demitrios had been professionally trained. The persistence of these rumors eventually compelled the doctors who conducted the autopsy to conclude their report with the words, "The wounds were not inflicted by an expert, but were in fact perfectly ordinary* for such an attack."

It did not take long after his return to Pretoria in 1963 for things to go badly between Mimis and his family. Initially he

---

*With peculiar insensitivity, the authors of the report used the Afrikaans word *doodgewoon*—i.e., "dead ordinary."

boarded with his half-brother, Victor. After just a few days, though, Victor had had enough. Demitrios was an eccentric, restless, troubling person to have in the house. He got up at 5:00 A.M. and stood next to his bed with his Bible open in his hand. He was convinced that his travels abroad had given him a wisdom the provincials around him lacked. He would give instructions to anyone he came across and made a habit of interfering in other people's business. That, at any rate, was his half-brother's view.

His stepmother and half-sister Evangelina also found him a handful. He would hold forth to them about his travels and about the Christian Church, with whose members in the Transvaal he had managed to make contact. It was difficult to make sense of much of what he said. Marika regretted bringing him back with her from Lourenço Marques. He could not accept the fact that he had not come into an inheritance. At meals he stuffed himself shamelessly. Marika's grandchildren laughed at the way he ate. They thought of him as a kind of hippopotamus who carried them about on his back, barked like a dog, and sometimes rode on his bike with them in the city parks. He was a remarkable sight on his bicycle. People stared at him. He was oversized and wore a Stetson.

A week after his arrival Demitrios was caught going through Marika's desks and drawers in search of his father's effects. Marika and Victor gave him some money and told him to be on his way.

For the next six months Demitrios worked as a welder and an odd-job man in Pretoria. He paid regular visits to his brother-in-law Nikos Vlachopoulus, who, with Demitrios's middle half-sister, Helena, managed the Proclamation Hill Cafe. He would spend hours there, reading the newspapers and receiving acquaintances as if he were holding audience with them. At the beginning of July his current employers, F. A. Poole (Pty.) Ltd., moved to an industrial area outside Pretoria. This move involved taking inventory, in the course of which Demitrios fell out with the foreman. Some days later he was fired. That same day he applied to the Ministry of External Affairs for an exit visa.

Demitrios felt optimistic about his future. His papers were in order, he could go where he liked, he could even think of himself as a kind of tourist in South Africa. In July 1964 he crossed the border into Rhodesia. He had fifty pounds in his pocket. In Maradellas, near Salisbury, he visited his sister Katerina, now Mrs. Pnevma. Her husband was unpleasantly surprised by the arrival of this newfound half-brother, whom Katerina barely remembered: a man who had been rejected by the family and who brought with him an unpleasant reputation. An hour's conversation between them was enough. Demitrios was told to move on.

So he went to Nyasaland. From the capital, Blantyre, he traveled to Lake Nyasa in the company of a fish trader. Failing to find work there, he returned to Salisbury. At the end of August the police deported him on the grounds that his entry permit had expired. He used his Portuguese passport to return to Mozambique. The end of the year found him living in the town of Gondola and working for the Hume Pipe-laying Company.

•

On weekends Demitrios would drink a few glasses of beer with members of the local Greek community. They were impressed by his travels and his command of languages, but they also thought he talked a lot of nonsense, especially about Portugal's colonies. Sometimes he declaimed biblical texts. An Orthodox priest who visited Gondola from Umtali, in Rhodesia, spread the rumor that he was actually not a Greek but a Turk.

On one occasion he admitted to people he met at a hotel in Gondola that he was the black sheep of his family. When they appeared not to understand, Demitrios took off his hat and showed them the graying tight curls of his hair. "That's why they won't have me near them," he said. He declared that one day a complete mingling of the races would finally take place in Africa. Everyone then would be a bastard. They would all come together in bed, and God would find it good.

One member of his audience angrily banged his glass down on the table; the others burst out laughing.

On another occasion Demitrios was standing at the bar with a group of black employees of the Hume Company. He was in high spirits, speaking to them in their own language and, it seemed to others present, instructing them as though they were his disciples.

"This isn't going to last long," he shouted suddenly in Portuguese. "This country isn't Portugal—it's the United States of Mozambique."

The whites in the room pricked up their ears.

"Any day all this will come to an end. We mustn't be fooled into calling ourselves Portuguese here, because we're Africans. We'll have a blue flag. With a rainbow on it."

In southern Africa the rainbow was, and still is, the symbol of a multicolored society.

"Long live our country, the United States of Mozambique!" he cried.

The following day he was picked up by agents of the PIDE. He was taken to the port of Beira and handed over to the local commandant, Captain Luis Tavara. Subsequently he was interrogated by another officer, Inspector Horacio Ferreira.

A rainbow of races? The United States of Mozambique? How could he think of saying such things in public, in a Portuguese colony? This was subversive propaganda, political agitation, and worse.

Far from being cowed by these accusations, however, Demitrios told his interrogators that it was more than time that free elections were held in the country. He reminded them that he was working on the oil pipeline, a strategic asset essential to the economy and to the survival of the whites. The Portuguese administration had a monopoly on the supply of fuel to the colony, but only the whites were profiting from it.

Ferreira was determined to find out if this troublemaker had made contact with the terrorists of Frelimo, the Mozambique Liberation Front. Demitrios was kept for ten weeks in preventive detention. He asked for some of his books to be sent from Pretoria, so that he would have something to read and would be able to keep in touch with the members of the Christian Church in Durban and Cape Town.

By mid-January the investigation had led nowhere. The mendicant monks had been consulted; the headquarters of the PIDE in Lisbon had also turned in a report. The conclusions drawn about him were no different from those recorded in 1950, 1953, and 1962. Years had passed since Demitrios had been admitted to a psychiatric ward, but he was once again declared to be "fundamentally a psychopath." Ultimately, Inspector Ferreira found the ever-lengthening tale of his wanderings pointless and bewildering. At the end of January, he closed the dossier and let Demitrios go.

On 5 March 1965 Demitrios boarded the Indian passenger liner *Karanja*. The journey from Beira to Durban took just two days. On the morning of the eighth he was admitted to the Republic of South Africa. He came ashore with two suitcases and some cooking utensils in a cardboard box. He was never to leave the country again.

He rented a room in the central area of Durban and went to look for the Cuban Hat Tearoom, near the north beach. The owner of the tearoom, Kyriakos Skordis, had been recommended to him. Skordis had no work but told him he could use the place as a postal address. A few days later Demitrios came by to say that he had been registered at the local court as a translator in Greek and Portuguese. When he next visited the tearoom it was to report that he had got a job with the South African Railways. As he was obviously broke, the railways' personnel department advanced him some money and admitted him into a hostel for its employees. The work was tedious: he had to couple and uncouple the vacuum hoses connecting one carriage to another and do minor electrical repairs. After three weeks he had had enough. A week later he left his depressing hostel room, taking the Gideon Bible he had found in its chest of drawers. By then he had already managed to get himself a new position, in the little trading town of Mandini, a hundred kilometers north of Durban. He was going to work there as a fitter for the firm of Fraser & Chalmers Ltd.

In May, Demitrios was admitted to the hospital in Mandini with a severe stab wound in his left arm. He and a colleague, a fellow Greek by the name of Nikos Vergas, had argued in the Fraser & Chalmers canteen. Demitrios had knocked Vergas down but Vergas had come back at him with a knife he had drawn from his back pocket. The wound on Demitrios's arm was fourteen centimeters long. He brought charges against his attacker and both men appeared before the local magistrate a few days later. As the quarrel between them had been conducted in Greek throughout, none of the witnesses could say what it had been about. Demitrios volunteered to act as translator, but since he was a party to the case his offer was not accepted.

Case dismissed.

"Communist bastard," Vergas shouted after him, out in the street.

Some time after this incident Father Hanno Probst of the Roman Catholic mission to Zululand drove into Mandini.

He called at the post office, as he always did, and at the local general dealers in the main street. Leaving the store, he noticed a middle-aged man sitting in the sun on a bench. His left arm was swathed in a bandage. He was reading a newspaper. Probst was struck by his dejected expression.

The priest was from southern Germany. During the many years he had spent in South Africa he had acquired a sharp eye for the physical characteristics that distinguished the races: subtle gradations in pigmentation and bone structure, differences in the shape of the nose and the curl of the hair. He was proud of his refined powers of observation in this regard, especially as such indicators were of life-and-death significance in those days. To his eye the man with the injured arm was plainly a colored. He was convinced of it immediately. But he was sure, too, that he was not a South African.

"If you don't mind my asking, are you a Mozambican?"

The man looked up morosely.

"You're far from home, aren't you?"

"How do you know I come from there?"

"Oh, I've been around a lot. It's a hobby of mine, to guess where people come from."

The Mozambican moved up on the bench. He, too, had traveled a great deal, he said. Soon he was boasting to the stranger. Apart from English, he said, he knew seven languages. Probst tried him in Spanish and Italian. To his astonishment, the man spoke both languages fairly well; his Portuguese, not surprisingly, was fluent. Then there was his German, spoken, after some hesitation, with an unmistakable Bavarian accent.

Probst was amazed. What was a man with a command of these languages up to in this remote corner of Zululand?

"You must have had very good teachers in Moscow," the priest said suddenly, to throw the other man off balance.

"And you in Rome," the man answered after a short silence and with an odd turn in his voice.

Hanno Probst, who was dressed in mufti, admitted that he was indeed a Roman Catholic priest and that he lived at the mission station in the Mangete reserve, not far from a place called Mtunzini. They did a lot of good work there.

Suddenly excited, the man burst out: "You Catholics are all the same. Profiteers. Exploiters. Look at Salazar. Those little nuns in Mozambique—you know what they do? They pump insulin into the blacks. They think there are too many of them, so they just do away with them. And the Portuguese know all about it."

"You're a Communist," Probst cried out.

The Communist folded up his newspaper and casually strolled toward the gas station nearby.

The meeting left Probst nonplussed. Was he indeed a *métique,* he wondered, or a European? Either way, someone ought to be warned about him. The next morning he once again drove fifty kilometers along the coast road, from his mission station to Mandini. The little town did not have a police station, so he went instead to the security office of the biggest local factory, S. A. Pulp and Paper Industries on the Tugela River. The officials there listened attentively to his story. They assured the priest they would pass the information he had given them on to the police. Clearly the man was dangerous. One Nikos Vergas had been in to see them not long before, bearing much the same kind of information.

Demitrios picked up his mail at the Cuban Hat Tearoom toward the end of August. Among the items waiting for him was a note from Helen Daniels, a member of the Christian Church. She was a pious, single colored woman from Cape Town. She wrote that she was eager to get to know him; she had heard much about him from others. The possibility of marriage was not excluded.

That night Demitrios packed his bags once again.

In one big case he put the following: a brown suit, sweaters, a raincoat, two cream-colored jackets, underpants, socks, four handkerchiefs, twelve neckties, a pillowcase, two green sheets, a blue blanket, two hats, and various items of dirty laundry. Mixed up with these items were his books and papers, including: *Poems Old and New, The Concise Oxford English Dictionary, A Hebrew Grammar,* an *Afrikaans Exercise Book, Ogretmen not defteri* (property of the Tarhaban College, Istanbul), *An die Freunde Des Practical English, Compêndio da Gramátika Francesa, Gramática de Xisonga,* a map of Athens, the Gideon Society Bible he had taken from the railwayman's hostel, and a medical manual on intestinal disorders and acute stomach ulcers.

The other case contained a carpenter's square, two bolts, a can opener, needles, eleven keys, two rolls of cotton, a saw, two combs, a pair of welder's goggles, a pair of reading glasses, a little tin containing buttons, a pair of swimming trunks, a dishcloth, hairbrushes, two saucepans with lids, one saucepan without a lid, a toaster, a hammer, a file, a spirit level, two pairs of shoes, a plastic helmet, a spoon, a fork, two pairs of striped pajamas, a little pot of glue, a mirror, and a bar of soap.

Demitrios set off the next day. Having arranged a lift with a traveling salesman as far as Port Elizabeth, he loaded all his gear into the trunk of a Ford sedan. From Port Elizabeth he continued his journey by rail. After two days his train stopped under the elaborate Victorian iron roof of Cape Town's main railway station. He was back in the city he had left in 1942. He felt that there was something not quite right inside him. It was as if he had a slight fever. Or as if a hunger of an unfamiliar kind were gnawing at him.

Sometimes one cannot help wishing that everything over the centuries had been captured on film. In Technicolor. With each life a small segment of the entire show. Who would be able to turn his gaze away from Demitrios Tsafendas, newly arrived at the main Cape Town railway station, carrying two suitcases containing a bundle of dirty linen and a collection of pots, pans, and cutlery?

But were one truly in a position to watch such a film, which moments would one actually choose to witness? In all of Tsafendas's tormented career, his assault in the House of Assembly, which took place a year and nine days after his arrival in Cape Town, might seem almost inconsequential or marginal. Would one necessarily choose to witness a thirty-year-old murder if one could instead hear again the long-silent shuffle on linoleum of two pairs of shoes in a nondescript house in the suburb of Bellville South? It was there, in the front room of the house, in the middle of the Cape winter, that Tsafendas met for the first time the woman who had indicated to him that she wished to become his wife. Helen

Daniels was thirty-five years old. How did they greet each other? What did they say next?

Her father and brother had gone in their car to the station, where they had picked him up. Helen knew nothing about Demitrios, other than that he had traveled the world and he was a member of the fellowship, the Christian Church, to which she and her family belonged. She had written two or three letters to him earlier in the winter and had also sent a snapshot of herself, asking him to do the same. But the request had been ignored. In the end, she knew only his handwriting. Demitrios wrote his letters with a fountain pen, in a strikingly elegant, self-assured, un–South African hand. From what he had actually put down little information emerged.

When he made a flesh-and-blood appearance at the gate to the front garden and then advanced toward the door of her parents' home, Helen didn't like the look of him. He had a double chin. She had imagined him less stout. He was unshaven; there were holes in his jersey; his bags—those battered suitcases—made him look like some kind of hawker carrying his goods from door to door. Still, this out-of-luck peddler had good manners. Demitrios took a seat. He drank his tea and began to tell his tales. He had served on American warships and had once been torpedoed. He knew Europe like the palm of his hand. He had been in Palestine and visited the holy places and wandered along the banks of the Jordan. That he spilled some of his tea in his saucer, Helen felt, should not be held against him.

When her father began to pray and sing hymns, after they had drunk their tea, Demitrios joined in fervently. Obviously there was nothing amiss with his faith. He was shown the little room that had been set aside for him. It was agreed he would lodge temporarily with them on Sans Souci Street. They knew that on his identity card their lodger was registered as a white; they were therefore breaking the law in letting him stay under their roof.

Helen was left feeling ill at ease about her suitor. Her distrustful glances had not escaped him, though his stories about the Middle East, about his Greek father and his natural mother had softened the first, rather unfavorable impression he had made on her. He had let it be understood that henceforth he planned to live his life as a colored. He wanted to get a new identity card, one without the *W* before and after his name and number, which indicated that he had been accepted as a member of the "white population group." He was determined to see to the matter immediately.

The word *marriage* was uttered by neither of them. Both felt embarrassed by it.

The following day Demitrios went to the Population Registration Office and handed in his identity card. He wanted to be registered as a colored, he said. That required his making a formal declaration, as stipulated in the Population Registration Act. The declaration was drafted in the usual terms: Demitrios Tsafendas regards himself as a colored, lives in a colored residential area, has the intention of entering into marriage with a woman of mixed racial origin.

The bureaucratic mills were to grind slowly over this request. Applications were flooding in from coloreds who wanted to be classified as whites. Applications to change from white to colored were rare indeed. Demitrios was one of the exceedingly small number of people who were volunteering to disadvantage themselves by crossing in that particular direction the crazy, artificial boundary between races.

For six weeks he remained with the Daniels family. During that time he heard nothing from the Population Registration Office. He wondered why his reclassification was taking so long. In the meantime he had managed to get a job as a fitter in a local power station. Perhaps, Mr. Daniels suggested, he might make a contribution to the costs of the household, as the family's means were limited. Demitrios now began to complain of stomach pains. At mealtimes he would withdraw from the table, grimacing, and head for his room.

Still nothing had been said about marriage. At forty-seven he was quite old for Helen; she was twelve years younger. In the end, relieved that he kept silent on the subject, she decided to let the prospect of marriage between them quietly evaporate. He was a charming man, she thought, and she enjoyed listening to his opinions on various subjects, but his behavior increasingly struck her as odd. At night he would go into the kitchen and hunt around for something to eat. She had once found him on his bed with his shoes on.

"He was just lying there with his feet on the bedspread," Helen complained. It was a fluffy, rose-colored bedspread made of combed cotton.

•

During September and October 1965 Demitrios went regularly to meetings of the Christian Church. These meetings took place in various houses all over the Cape Peninsula. In the whole western Cape there were about eight hundred people in the group. Their church did not have a building of its own, gave out no reading matter, and did not hold collections during its services. The Gospel was presented in an informal, friendly manner; the transforming power of Christ's presence was proclaimed; tea or a light supper was shared after the service. The community abided strictly by the law. In the words of one of its leaders: "Our faith caters for European and non-European races. We are not multiracial, but we do gather with colored members of the Christian Church during our annual conferences. We, however, obey the apartheid laws. By this I mean that the members of different races eat and sleep separately."

It made no difference to Demitrios whether the services he attended took place in colored areas or in the better-off white neighborhoods. He went back and forth between them as the spirit moved him. His white fellow believers formed the impression that he came to the services chiefly for the food. He appeared devout but was ignorant of the texts. He sat with his hands on his knees. Sometimes his legs could be seen trembling. And he called for the discussion of strange questions. How, for instance, could Jesus have been active in heaven before appearing in Mary's womb? He sang hymns with the enthusiasm of a child; this went over better among the coloreds than among the whites.

One day, after a Bible reading, he was taken aside by James

Johnson, a white elder of the community. This was the second time the man had questioned him. What exactly was the color of his skin, Johnson wanted to know. As determined from the official point of view, of course. Was he a Greek or a "nonwhite"? Demitrios began to explain his circumstances. Johnson interrupted him. As long as his racial classification was officially white ("European")—surely this must be clear to him?—he should no longer go to prayer meetings in the houses of coloreds. Nothing but trouble would come of it.

Toward the beginning of the Cape summer Demitrios left Bellville South. He wandered from one rented room to another in the city center, ending up in the south, in Lansdowne, where a family by the name of O'Ryan offered him shelter. Patrick O'Ryan, whom he had met at one of the meetings of the Christian Church, was a teacher at Bishop Lavis High School. He took pity on the homeless Greek. He shared with him not only his bread and his belief but also a mixed background. It was apparent to him that Demitrios had only a limited understanding of the Bible, but for the rest he found him easy to get on with.

Demitrios remained unemployed for several weeks. He applied for a job as a concierge at the French embassy, in vain, and for a clerkship at Groote Schuur Hospital, with the same result. Soon after the New Year he tried for a job as a conductor on the city tramways but had no success there either—he was too heavy to run up and down the narrow stairs of a double-decker all day. Next he applied to the Marine Diamond Corporation, a company with headquarters in the harbor. On 13 January 1966 he successfully underwent a medical examination; two weeks later he was at work.

The company dredged for diamonds on the Atlantic coast. Demitrios sailed on a supply ship for a site six hundred miles north of Table Bay, at the mouth of the Orange River. He and the other workmen on board spent a night getting there; then they were transferred to a dinghy with an outboard motor. A strong southeaster was blowing. With difficulty the dinghy reached the giant pontoon on which the dredging machine was mounted. While the others were still vomiting over the railings or were taking to their bunks below, Demitrios, exhausted though he was, went to the bathroom and prepared for the day ahead.

The foreman at once decided that this man "knew the sea." The crew worked twelve-hour shifts for twenty days at a time; then they were sent for ten days' leave in Cape Town. At first Demitrios fit in well. Though lazy, he was seldom sick; he ate like an ox and generally slept about three hours less when off shift than the rest of the men. Together with John Hulse, a student earning money during his vacation, and an older American crewman, he maintained the pumps that sucked up mud from the sea bottom and transferred it into giant bins.

Demitrios talked nonstop while on the job; it was as if being back on the ocean, even in these circumstances, had loosened his tongue. In no time at all everyone knew all about his *Wanderjahre* and his contempt for the South African regime. He was proud of having spent time living among

Malays and coloreds. You could get on with such people, he announced; at least they had some sense. The Nationalist Party was crap and wouldn't last long. As for the Immorality Act—which forbade love between the races—it was the act itself that was immoral, not what it tried to prevent.

The head of security on board, a man named Keith Martincich, warned Demitrios to put more distance between himself and the black riggers and unskilled workers on board the dredger; also to keep away from the filters through which the mud was sieved. Quite apart from mud and diamonds, the pumps sucked up quantities of red lobsters. Demitrios, the seafood lover, could not keep away from such a bonanza. In free moments during the night shift he would fish about in the bins and then, in the mornings, bring his harvest into the kitchen.

Martincich was a slightly built man of twenty-three. He decided to watch this odd fellow and crept after him whenever he took himself to some deserted corner of the deck. To his surprise, he heard the man, at these times, talking loudly to himself. It was a long monologue—or was it a dialogue? Demitrios spoke of himself as a man who had dived into the sea to rescue drowning men. He acted out the story of the Cape hero Wolraad Woltemade, who rode on horseback to bring shipwrecked sailors ashore.

In his mind, Demitrios was listening attentively once again to the English mistress at his school in Middelburg. Lost in these reveries, he clapped his hands and cried out loudly. Then he would fall silent and stare at the strip of land visible in the distance. He felt an inexplicable sadness. He longed for

Mozambique, for Cora in her house of many rooms. And still further back too, for Alexandria and his grandmother Katerina, who had always treated him so kindly. The sun went down. The mud from the broad mouth of the Orange River streamed out to sea, turning the water blood-brown.

Two months later Demitrios appeared in the Cape Town office of Gillian Liebermann, head of personnel for the Marine Diamond Corporation. The noise and vibration on board the great dredger had damaged his hearing, he told her. His nose was troubling him too; this was an aftereffect of having had it broken six years before, in a fight in a Jerusalem slum. In Liebermann's opinion his clothing and physical appearance were not those of the average employee of the Marine Diamond Corporation. His hat and his European-style suit made him something of an exception, an oddity. He struck her as a unique and imaginative person. She questioned him, listened to his stories, and found herself drawn into a long conversation with him. The upshot of their meeting was an appointment with the firm's medical officer.

At the beginning of April he took two weeks' leave and was admitted to Groote Schuur Hospital. Dr. Leon Goldmann, an ear, nose, and throat specialist, operated on his left nostril. Three days later he was discharged. A social worker took him from the hospital to a boardinghouse run by a former nurse in the suburb of Observatory.

Demitrios shared his room with an Afrikaans-speaking bus driver and a German backpacker. When, at the end of one of the meals they took together, he politely thanked the black maid who had served at their table, he saw the Afrikaner scowl. This led to a heated argument between them about Verwoerd, the blacks, and the bantustans supposedly being developed for them. The tension between Demitrios and his roommate deepened over the next few days. Demitrios refused to put out his bedside lamp at night; he insisted on reading into the small hours. He slept with his money and papers hidden under his pillow. On the last day of May he told the owner of the boardinghouse, to her face, that the Afrikaners were a backward people. She responded by telling him to go look for lodgings elsewhere.

He must have felt particularly hopeless during those months of 1966. Again he went from rented room to rented room, this time in that flat stretch of the city that lies just below Devil's Peak. He applied for one menial job after another, never with any success. Now and then he went back to the Population Registration Office to record his changes of address so that he could be informed if his application to alter his racial status had been granted. The papers, he was told, had been sent to the Ministry of the Interior in Pretoria, where they were being carefully studied. Continuous headaches and dizziness led Demitrios to seek help from a neurologist, but nothing emerged from the examination. He was told that he was suffering from a form of migraine and that he was over-weight—nothing else. The doctor sent him away with some codeine tablets and a pamphlet on dieting. Because of his gross appetite and table manners, Demitrios had become notorious in the rundown café where he usually took his lunch, on the edge of District Six. The people working there had given him a nickname: "The Pig."

During one of his many visits to the labor bureau, Demitrios fell into conversation with a retired railwayman. The railwayman told him that casual jobs could often be found in the Senate and the House of Assembly. As the government migrated seasonally between Cape Town and Pretoria, the officials who ran the day-to-day business of parliament were always looking for temporary messengers and suchlike. The pay was poor. Jobs of that sort should have been filled by coloreds, really, but the dignity of parliament demanded otherwise. A temporary position there would be better than nothing, anyway.

On Monday, 18 July, Demitrios appeared for a short interview in the parliament building. He had cut his hair for the occasion and shaved himself with special care. He wore a gray suit. He was received in an impressive wood-paneled office by the chief messenger, Mr. Burger, who was accompanied by two senior messengers, Schuin and Wiehahn.

First of all, they told him, he must not expect a permanent job, for reasons he already knew. The work itself was not onerous: mostly it consisted of sorting mail and delivering messages, documents, and newspapers. He would have to be obedient to his superiors. At the end of the Cape session, in three months' time, he would be discharged. Schuin lit a cigarette. Wiehahn stirred his coffee. Burger asked him if he understood the position.

Demitrios answered that he did indeed. A number of

formal questions were then rapidly put to him. Was he a South African? Could he prove that he was classified as a white? What grade had he reached at school? Who were his previous employers? When had he been discharged from their employ?

The officials examined the certificate of attendance he had received from the Middelburg School, as well as the registration card issued by the labor bureau, on which his identity-card number (with its *W* for white) also appeared. They listened to his account of working for the Marine Diamond Corporation and did not question the reason he gave for resigning: "On account of age." Demitrios added that he had also worked at one time as a court translator in Natal.

"Did you really translate from Greek and Portuguese in front of a magistrate?" Wiehahn asked, after Demitrios listed his languages for them. Burger, who had been watching him closely, said in Afrikaans to the other two, "I don't think we can use someone like this as a messenger."

Demitrios turned toward him. "I understand what you're saying, sir. But I'm hungry. I'm desperate. I need the job."

"You should be looking for something better," the chief messenger told him. "We have trouble with people like you."

Burger had a poor opinion of most of those who came to his door in search of a job. A spineless lot they were. Unemployed youngsters, fired railwaymen, marginal types. The law compelled him to hire whites only, but what kind of whites would choose such work? Rubbish, the sweepings of the slums. Or else older and better-educated men who would take off at the first opportunity. As far as he was concerned, it was the latter category to which Tsafendas belonged.

"Yes, we do have trouble with people like you," Schuin joined in. "You're here for a day or two and then you're gone."

Demitrios promised he would stay for the full three-month period.

Schuin and Wiehahn nodded politely in the direction of the door. Tsafendas took the hint. Other applicants were waiting in the anteroom. He would be informed by mail whether he had got the job or not.

Three days later the Greek oil tanker *Eleni,* en route to the Persian Gulf, lost a section of its rudder. It wallowed help-lessly in the Atlantic Ocean, to the southeast of the Cape of Good Hope, until a Portuguese trawler responded to Captain Michaelis Fountatos's call for help. The *Eleni* was towed into Table Bay and moored at the Duncan Dock on Sunday evening, 24 July.

Demitrios always followed the newspaper column devoted to the comings and goings of ships in and out of the port. On Monday evening he went on board the *Eleni.* He spent a couple of hours with the ship's cook and others, introducing himself to them as a fellow seaman. Later that evening they offered him a place at their mess table.

The entire crew of the *Eleni* was Greek. The boat would have to spend weeks in dry dock while its rudder was being repaired. Any diversion was welcome. Demitrios told his newfound friends about the shows in town. If they wanted to buy clothes or anything else he knew where to take them.

Thereafter he appeared on the *Eleni* for lunch every day. After all, he was a Greek among fellow Greeks once again. He accompanied members of the crew when they went ashore and introduced them to Mike Augustides of Mike's Outfitters, who was eager to do business with them. He also took them to a bar in Woodstock where the booze was cheap and then to the little lanes in District Six and Walmer where the whores plied their trade. A number of the men had visited the Cape previously and had fond memories of the high quality of its *dagga* and the good looks of its colored women. But Mimis warned them to be careful. Some of the police might wink an eye at what went on but, in general, magistrates dealt harshly with people brought up before them. For a white man to have sex with a colored woman could lead to a month or more in jail. His friends shrugged their shoulders at this. What was forbidden by day was hidden at night. Besides, one of them said, everybody knew that this Verwoerd was himself married to a colored woman. She had passed, or her mother had passed. So now she was white.

The watchman on the *Eleni* was an Afrikaner by the name of Stollenkamp. He was on the alert even during the small hours of the night, when the seamen would try to smuggle their women up the gangway. "No coloreds on board," he insisted fiercely.

On 1 August Demitrios took up his duties as a parliamentary messenger. Schuin and Wiehahn gave him his instructions.

He was attached to the press and information division of the House. A blue uniform was issued to him, along with a set of khaki-colored overalls and a locker in which to keep his belongings. Most of his time was passed in a basement lobby. It was there that the messengers waited. They were summoned to different rooms in the buildings by lights on a panel fixed to the wall. He had to take tea or coffee to members of parliament and visiting journalists and carry bundles of papers from one place or person to another.

Thus, to his own bewilderment, Demitrios Tsafendas found himself, day after day, close to some of the most powerful people in the country: ministers, parliamentary representatives from near and far, the bigwigs of the governing Nationalist Party and the opposition. In the poorer quarters of the city anyone who was acquainted with him knew how much he detested Verwoerd and his Nationalists. Yet, through some freakish mischance, here he was, at the very center of the country's political life. Among them, surrounded by them, yet as if invisible.

The irony of his holding a position just there, at that place and at that particular moment, was even greater than he could have known. His request to be reregistered as a colored under the Population Registration Act—a request he had initiated eleven months earlier—had been passed from office to office in the Ministry of the Interior in Pretoria until, some time in July 1966, it had been discovered that the name of the applicant appeared on the blacklist of those forbidden to enter South Africa. On 8 August, the secretary of the interior submitted to his minister an order for Demitrios's deportation. The order was signed by the minister the next day and dispatched to Cape Town. On Friday, 2 September, a low-ranking official in Cape Town finally got around to typing a letter informing Tsafendas that he was to be deported. The letter remained in the official's out tray until the day of the murder.

Who can tell when Demitrios decided to carry out an action that would heal his past or make it whole? Was it in Durban, when he returned to South Africa? Or when the Catholic priest in Mandini accosted him?

He was sick with shame and nostalgia. Nostalgia for he knew not what. Between the women of his mind and the women he met there was a gulf that nothing could bridge. He had worn out the soles of his shoes looking for companionship on the streets of Cape Town; but no sooner did he find someone to talk to than another face, a face from the past, came between him and his interlocutor. Everything he remembered melted into everything else. It was as if another person were walking alongside him, always just out of step. Sometimes he seemed to be ahead of his companion, sometimes behind. Even the thoughts he had, his own thoughts, seemed to well up inside this other person. Always he felt himself to be on a journey from one place to another or from one place that strangely substituted itself for another. Now his imaginings ran together, unstoppably, violently, indiscriminately, filling him with shame; now they put before him, with a shameless reality far stronger than anything present and concrete, precise moments from his past.

During the weekends of August Demitrios could no longer bear to leave his room. The toilet was at the end of a corridor, but it was impossible for him to negotiate even that distance. When he was sure his landlady was not around, he peed into cola bottles and threw them out the window, into the garden. He ate chocolate bars incessantly, one after the other, a whole bar at a time. His room was littered with their silver wrappings.

When he finally understood what he was going to do, what he had to do, when the deed made itself known to him, he felt a kind of relief, as if all the turmoil in his mind were suddenly stilled. In its place came an emptiness. It was impossible for him to tell whether it was agreeable or not.

What could be easier, now that he had a job in parliament? Everything was at hand. He had long believed that a firearm was the most efficient weapon a man could use to kill another. A revolver or pistol had the great advantage of striking from a distance and therefore of allowing the assailant to escape. Previously he had had no idea what "escape" might mean, but now that the *Eleni* lay in the harbor the answer seemed clear. Once one was inside the parliament building, he knew, security was very lax. He would come on the man in one of the corridors, shoot him, escape in the confusion that was bound to follow, and run like hell toward the docks.

But time was running short: the *Eleni* was due to sail within a few days. He had become very tight with some of the members of the crew. They often complained to him about the stupidity of South African laws. He allowed himself to drop some vague hints of what he had in mind and they encouraged him to go ahead—or so it seemed to him. He even set a definite date for carrying out his plan: 2 September. Manolis, the tall bosun on the *Eleni,* told him that he had a Beretta that he would part with for eighty dollars.

On 1 September, Demitrios went to the Adderley Street branch of Barclays Bank. He produced his passport and bought American dollars. Then he took a taxi to the docks. He greeted the man on day watch and went below. But now that Manolis realized Demitrios was in earnest, he suddenly got cold feet. The two men began to shout at each other. Manolis took him into the kitchen, knowing that the cook's assistant, a seventeen-year-old named Nikolas Mavronas, had a small pistol he wanted to dispose of. Mavronas brought it out for them to see, a black weapon with a white butt and an inscription: BREVETTATA .22 MADE IN ITALY. Mavronas did not have any ammunition. Mimis finally counted out thirty dollars and left the boat with the gun in his pocket.

Manolis saw him off the side and told the watchman not to let him on board again—the man was crazy. The watchman did not take this instruction seriously. The fat fellow had been coming and going all month long, without doing any harm, and was obviously on good terms with some of the men.

That evening, in his room in Aldor Apartments, Rondebosch, Mimis discovered that the gun was little more than a toy. It was a small-caliber gas pistol, barely a firearm at all. He swallowed his anger as best he could. He consulted his Bible but got no guidance from it.

The following day he carried out in a distracted fashion the jobs he was given to do. Sent into town to dispatch a message for one of the parliamentary correspondents, he came back with the wrong change. That evening the press corps gave its annual party for members of the Senate and the House of Assembly. Demitrios was asked to help out as a waiter. One of the guests at the party was John Hulse, a member of the Students Representative Council at Cape Town University and a friend of an opposition M.P. He recognized Demitrios and greeted him warmly. They'd worked together on that dredger; didn't he remember? Demitrios gave him an evasive answer.

On Saturday, 3 September, he went on board the *Eleni* for the last time. He wanted to get back his thirty dollars. Either that or another gun. Or even a decent knife. Manolis and the cook's assistant told him that they'd spent the money and it was too late now to ask for it back.

"Piss off," the bosun said. "What do you think we are, a couple of cowboys?"

Nevertheless Demitrios ate in the galley with them and some others. At three o'clock he went onto the bridge, where Michaelis Fountatos was preparing for the boat's departure. Demitrios complained to the captain that he'd been swindled, but the captain simply hustled him off the bridge. He should settle his own accounts with the men below.

At six o'clock that evening the ropes that moored the *Eleni* to the quay were cast off.

....

At a quarter to seven on the morning of Tuesday, 6 September—it was a clear spring day—Demitrios took up his position in the lobby of the House of Assembly. He wasn't expected on duty for another hour, and he occupied himself with the morning newspapers. Over the weekend Verwoerd had held a meeting with Chief Leaboa Jonathan, the leader of Basutoland, a former British protectorate. Today at two the prime minister was expected to report on the meeting and to make an important statement on the future of the bantustans. Parliament would be full, Mimis knew. Almost all the members would want to be present, not to speak of the public seeking admission to the gallery.

There was no way back for him.

He left for the city center before nine. In one shop, William Rawbone's, he bought a dagger. Five minutes later, in City Guns on Hout Street, he bought another, larger knife. The owner of City Guns took him to be a fisherman or a sailor and asked no questions. He wandered over to Greenmarket Square and fifteen minutes later returned to his post in the messengers' waiting room. No one had noticed his absence. By the time he resumed his usual place, he had deposited the knives in his locker. He had tied their scabbards to a belt that he concealed under his blue uniform jacket. Then he served tea to the reporters in their room on the first floor.

By two o'clock, just before the bell rang for the sitting to begin, the crowd that had gathered under the portico of the building was even bigger than he had expected. Some four hundred people were heading for the House of Assembly, among them the final-year students of the Afrikaans medium school, Du Preez Hoërskool, in the city's northern suburbs. Mimis went downstairs to pick up his knives and hide them under his jacket.

At ten past two Verwoerd made his appearance. He was accompanied by his personal bodyguard, Lieutenant Colonel Buytendag, and his private secretary. Demitrios stood among the crowd in the entrance, fumbling with his jacket as Verwoerd passed by. He followed the crowd into the House of Assembly. Buytendag turned and went up to the gallery. In a moment the prime minister would take his seat on the bench.

Demitrios approached him. He had managed to free one of his knives from its scabbard. He leaned forward. People assumed that he had a message to give to Verwoerd. Then he struck. His entire weight went into the blow. The blade disappeared into Verwoerd's chest, buried up to the hilt. The premier's upper body rose; it was a reflex response merely, not a defensive movement. Demitrios remained motionless for a moment, leaning over. He pulled the knife out. It could now be seen by the people around him. He stabbed the man yet again, three more times, before he was overpowered.

Everyone was screaming. A group of men had thrown the murderer on the floor. He was dragged over the benches, struck, stamped on, kicked.

Dr. Matthys Venter, a dominie of the Dutch Reformed Church and the M.P. for Kimberley District, was holding Demitrios's right arm. The knife was still clenched in his fist.

With something more than a clergyman's strength, Venter managed to force his fingers open and take the weapon from him. While others struggled to hold the assassin, Venter carefully laid the knife on the speaker's table. P. W. Botha, a cabinet minister, later to become president, rushed over to Helen Suzman, the solitary representative of the Progressive Party. His eyes bulging, his arms flailing, he thrust his fat forefinger in her face. "It's you who did this!" he shouted. "It's you liberals! Now we'll get you! We'll get the lot of you!"

Verwoerd's lifeless body was taken to Groote Schuur Hospital. An autopsy would have to be held to establish the precise cause of death. For all intents and purposes the prime minister had died at the moment of attack. He had stab wounds in his right shoulder, his right upper arm, and between his ribs; one of the thrusts had pierced his lung to a depth of thirteen centimeters and entered the right chamber of his heart.

Tsafendas was taken in a police van directly to the police station in Caledon Square, around the corner from the parliament building.

At a quarter to three, at the request of the police, he was examined by the district surgeon, Dr. R. Kossew. Demitrios had sustained bruised ribs and a cut along his eyebrow and the bridge of his nose. His shirt was covered with blood. Looking at him more closely, the doctor realized that his nose was broken; also that he had seen this man before. Two months earlier he had come to see him in connection with an application for a war pension. Kossew had thought him to be in a manifestly unstable state. Indeed, though he was not a psychiatrist, Kossew had jotted down the word *schizophrenic* in his notes.

Eventually Demitrios followed the prime minister's body to Groote Schuur. The wound on his brow was stitched up and his nose was put in a cast. He was also given an anti-tetanus injection.

Four hours after the attack he was taken to the office of Dr. I. Sakinofsky, the hospital's head of psychiatry.

There were just three people in the room, Dr. Sakinofsky, his assistant, and Demitrios. Sakinofsky asked him to lie down and try to relax.

Could he remember what had happened? Was it true that he had killed the prime minister?

Demitrios looked at him with an air of surprise. "I don't remember what happened afterward, but yes, I did stab him right through."

"What made you do a thing like that?"

"I didn't agree with the policy . . ."

Demitrios sat up. He put his face in his hands and burst into tears. He cried for some time. A flood of words, of broken sentences, followed. The doctor could make sense of few of them.

"Why are you crying?" he asked at one point.

"I don't know."

"Aren't you pleased with what you've done?"

"Yes. I'm glad to speak to you . . . someone better-class. I'm always among the poorer class of people."

Sakinofsky asked about his background. He listened attentively to the story Demitrios began to tell him.

"Why have you never married?"

Demitrios looked embarrassed; he even blushed. "I was working in a defense plant in Johannesburg when the war broke out. Then I joined an Allied convoy. I was very weak. I broke down after three months at sea. I didn't know then that I was troubled in my nerves . . . I see things, because of high blood pressure, coils and springs in front of my eyes. I hear no voices."

"Does God speak to you sometimes?"

Demitrios shook his head.

"Not personally. Only when I am in bed, fast asleep. Then I feel something that passes me by."

"Are your thoughts normal?"

"They are too rapid. In Portugal they brainwashed me and put alternating current in my head. Since then I have lost my faculties."

"Who are you against now?"

"I'm against Verwoerd. He's a foreigner . . . He is a Nationalist and he hasn't got the people behind him. I see no progress for the African people. There *is* something spiritual in me . . . I thought this thing had gone too far, they have made an ideology of it. The sexual part of it too—the Immorality Act, telling you who you can't marry . . . The only girl who wanted to marry me did not have the right identity card. I could not keep changing my identity card."

Then, after a short pause, "What do they actually say over the radio about the prime minister?"

"That he was stabbed to death in parliament."

"I remember stabbing him."

Sakinofsky noted that Demitrios answered his questions spontaneously. He seemed to look at what had happened from a distance, as if astonished that he had done something that had created such an uproar.

"What did you feel when you committed the murder?"

"Nothing. I just went blank."

The euphoria produced by South Africa's first truly national election in 1994—an election in which all races took part on equal terms—did not last long. Yes, a degree of human dignity had at last been restored to the country's blacks. But it soon began to dawn on them that their poverty was not going to disappear, nor were the glaring disparities between the housing and health care available to them and that enjoyed by most whites. As for the coloreds, they feared that a black African government might treat them with as much contempt as had their white masters. Among the whites a reluctant optimism and a feeling of collective guilt gave way to amnesia, indifference, defeatism. The hope that violence would cease now that the politics of the country were so changed was soon belied. In the countryside, larger numbers of Afrikaner farmers were being murdered than ever before; in the cities, where random killings went on unabated, it was as if the struggle had never ended. Indeed, far from being over, it seemed that the revolution that had

been feared or dreamed of for so long was only now beginning.

Thirty years after the murder of Verwoerd I found myself in
Krugersdorp, a gold-mining town about fifty kilometers west
of Johannesburg. Walking down the main street, I thought to
myself: Well, it had to happen. The harvest of the last many
years had been gathered. The self-confidence of the whites
had simply broken, in public at least. Or so it appeared. They
looked shabbier than before, the blacks more prosperous. Perhaps this impression sprang from the dress and carriage of
each group as it went about its business. The whites I saw in
Krugersdorp, barely an hour's drive from Johannesburg, wore
hideously ugly shorts, acrylic shirts, baseball caps with dirty bills.
Some of them even went barefoot. They slouched along,
without style, without self-regard. Did they imagine that
their lack of decorum signified some kind of sportiness? Was
this what "going native" entailed? Or did it spring simply
from a degree of poverty new to them? Yet the blacks around
them, who were poorer still, did not create the same impression. They tried to dress up, not down, as the whites did. For
the blacks there appeared to be something festive about going
to the city center—hence their polished shoes, Victorian hats,
party dresses, striped trousers and suits, bright umbrellas. The
last of these items gave warning of the thunderstorm that
would break out later in the day; such storms came regularly
on summer afternoons here in Gauteng (formerly known as
the Transvaal).

As if from long ago, from the old, old days, "poor whites"

had reappeared. They looked exactly like those I remembered only too well from the districts next to the suburban railway lines of my youth. In Krugersdorp they lived in an industrial area to the west of the town; their dilapidated rows of little houses ran alongside a polluted tributary of the Magalies River. The whole area stank of chemicals. All Afrikaans-speaking, all unemployed, all dependent on welfare handouts, they were rich only in the numbers of their children. But for how long, in the new South Africa, could they be sure of regularly receiving their benefit payments? They were precisely the people whom apartheid had privileged; now they glanced around shiftily—lost, not knowing what to look for next or where to look for it. They had been abandoned, here in Africa.

The old magistrates' court had been turned into a modest museum. Laid out as if in a series of shop windows were a variety of predictable items: geological specimens, mining gear, souvenirs of the Anglo-Boer War. (In the year 1900 about a thousand Boer women and children had died near the town in one of the concentration camps set up by the British.) At the back, on a windowsill, stood four bronze heads that made a deeper impression on me than all the other objects on display: the dust-covered heads of the successive leaders of the Nationalist Party. There they were, prime ministers all in their day: Hannes Strydom, Hendrik Verwoerd, B. J. Vorster, P. W. Botha.

Thirty years had passed since the second of these had been assassinated. What remained of that event? After almost three decades of imprisonment in Pretoria, Tsafendas had been removed to a psychiatric hospital some ten kilometers from the museum where I stood gazing at the portrait, cast in bronze, of his victim. Would it be possible to visit him? My fax to the Sterkfontein Hospital had been addressed—ah, the irony—to a Dr. Botha, the director, and to a Dr. Vorster, the chief physician. Now I had to wait for a few days: killing time in Krugersdorp.

Saturday afternoon in the hotel bar. Four fans turning above the pool table. The Rolling Stones emanating from the sound system. The room dark, the conversations loud.

A young woman turns and shouts at me, "I want to go barefoot, but just look at this filthy floor!" She has her arm around the shoulder of a man whose blue jeans hang below his belly. Below the cleft of his bottom, too.

She says: "I was seventeen when I had my first baby. It died. Then came this Boer, I went with this Boer. I was eighteen and I had his baby, the fucking arsehole, and at twenty still another one. If he gives me another baby I'm going to sell it for fucking *money*."

The girl behind the counter undoes the buttons of her blouse, to loud applause. She laughs at us, delighted with her success. The man with the exposed backside heads toward the toilet. The young mother turns to me again.

"Ach, pardon me," she says. "I just can't find a man worth loving. All they know is to stick it in and pump, stick it in and pump."

•

From the window of my room on the second floor of the hotel I could see the line of hills behind which, I knew, lay Sterkfontein Hospital. I felt that down in the Cape I would have been better able to assess my chances of success. In the Transvaal everything was different, on a bigger scale, less accessible. It was almost like being in another country, one that had little or nothing in common with the one I had left behind. For Transvaalers, of course, things were exactly the other way around. Table Mountain looked unreal to them; the blue of the Cape skies was like a curse.

Now that my obsession with Tsafendas was coming to its climax, I could no longer remember where it had begun. A long time ago I had decided that I had little to ask of the aged Demitrios. Nevertheless I felt a shrinking from the prospect of seeing him, a fear of doing so, as if I were about to step into icy water. Seventy-eight years old, for many years maltreated and tormented in Pretoria Central prison—the guards, I knew, used to spit in his food and piss in his coffee—he deserved now precisely what I could perhaps offer him, a little friendship of the Greek kind: they call it *paréa*. A handshake, a walk in the garden of the institution, a few calming words, nothing more.

Early on Monday morning I picked up the phone and called the hospital. After speaking to a few intermediaries I was put through to Dr. Vorster. Yes, she had received my fax. Her voice was neutral, distant. I told her, in Afrikaans, that I had been informed by the Ministry of Justice that permission from the medical authorities was necessary before a visit to Tsafendas could be arranged. Was that correct? Dr. Vorster coolly switched to English. Yes, the decision was in the hands of the hospital and in principle there was no objection. But they could not consent to my coming to see him now.

Then, with an unmistakable firmness of tone: "He is physically in no state to receive visitors."

Dr. Vorster proved to be as good as her word. No objection was made to my application to see the patient when I tried again eighteen months later. Demitrios's health had improved. I traveled from Amsterdam with a fax in my pocket. "Visit to Mr. Tsafendas approved. Please contact Matron Geyer to confirm date and time." An hour after my plane arrived in Johannesburg, I was back in my room in the Krugersdorp hotel. I phoned the hospital immediately, only to learn that Matron Geyer had already gone home for the day. I left a message to say I would call her the following day.

That night I stayed in my room and watched television. Thirty-eight years earlier, to the day, a famous uprising against apartheid—the fiercest and most widespread the country had yet seen—had begun in Sharpeville. In the course of a single morning sixty-seven blacks had been shot dead in that small township. Now the event was memorialized as Human Rights Day. President Mandela appeared on the screen, along with Vice President Mbeki, attending a commemorative ceremony held somewhere upcountry. The Afrikaans poet Breyten Breytenbach, who had himself undergone imprisonment and exile as an opponent of the apartheid regime, succeeded the politicians on the screen. Human rights, he said, included language rights, which meant that Afrikaners were entitled still to express themselves in Afrikaans. Then it was the turn of Matthews Phosa, the eccentric premier of the province of Mpumulanga (formerly the Eastern Transvaal). He expressed outrage at the fact that the head of state, President Mandela, had been subpoenaed to give evidence in a court case involving the management committee of the South African Rugby Union. Trivial, stupid intrigues of that sort must be halted, Phosa insisted.

They all seemed alike to me. Mbeki, Breytenbach, Phosa, the president—they had all been exiles in their time, if Mandela's years of imprisonment on Robben Island were regarded as a form of banishment. They had all been scarred by long, enforced absences, followed by sudden returns to a place that in the intervening years had itself undergone far-reaching processes of transformation, even of dissolution. And there was something else they had in common: for all the differences between them, they all spoke in a manner that seemed to me recognizably South African. Recognizably patriarchal, too. Their words were delivered with a biblical weight that people elsewhere could no longer readily adopt. Only Mbeki spoke with some hesitation, allowing long, haphazard pauses to interrupt his delivery.

At the end of the program there was a news flash about a fight between two Cape Colored street gangs on the waterfront in Cape Town. One of the gangs was a vigilante outfit that called itself PAGAD (People against Gangsterism and Drugs); the name of the other was not given. Two people had been killed; their bodies were shown, swathed in blood-drenched sheets. Rain could be seen in the background; visible, too, was the silhouette of Devil's Peak, washed by the downpour. Beloved Devil's Peak.

What was it a friend had told me, when I had last been there, as we drove through the rain toward the university?

"You know the difference between a neurotic and psychotic? A neurotic builds castles in the air. A psychotic lives in them."

The next morning the sky was like a gleaming, oppressive dome over the town. The weather forecast was for a high of 36°C later in the day; there would be no breeze to mitigate it. Nevertheless, as I headed north in the taxi taking me in the direction of the hills and the hospital beyond them, the stillness became less stifling. The heat began to feel weightless somehow. The glow in the air thinned toward the horizon, as if you were looking into a dusty crystal.

The institution was a closed one. Fiercely so. A fence of a special South African–style barbed wire, adorned with razor-sharp blades, ran all around it. Then came a second fence, also several meters high. Between the two fences more barbed wire had been spread out horizontally, to fill in the space. Uniformed guards at the gate inspected us morosely and checked the vehicle. I had to enter my name into a register and to give my contact and the purpose of my visit. On the other side of the double fence a number of brick bungalows were randomly scattered among trees, each at a distance from the others. The road curved between them. People wandered over the slopes in escorted groups. White-uniformed nurses, scattered like scraps of paper against the green grass, kept to the shade.

Mr. Tsafendas, I was told in the front office of a bare administrative building, was to be found in Ward 12B. The sister in charge would show me the way; she would not be long. When she came into the office, Matron Geyer stretched out a friendly hand; for some reason her handshake made me feel a little shy. But there was no need for me to say anything. She led me to her car. As we walked together she told me that a dance for the patients was going to take place that evening. Ooh-la-la, when they had a party you had to go into hiding. Most of the patients were black; most of them were pleasant enough. The dances were major occasions. They really looked forward to them. They turned up the sound system so loud you felt your ears would burst—you'd do anything to get out of the room. Anyway, the smoke alone would drive you away.

Mrs. Geyer said all this cheerfully and spontaneously, with no hint of disapproval or condescension in her voice. I thought better of asking her exactly what kind of "smoke" she had in mind.

Ward 12B was a barracklike building divided into a number of dim, echoing rooms. We went down a long corridor at the end of which were a vestibule and a little reception office. I was shown into the latter. It contained four chairs grouped around a low table. A recess paneled in hardwood had a framed text stuck on one wall, the words of an oath written by Florence Nightingale. "I solemnly pledge," I read, "before

God and in the presence of this assembly to practice my life in purity . . ." The rest was hidden behind a yucca plant in a pot. A little table in a corner near the window bore an expiring fern. The place smelled of Lysol and old meals and of something unpleasant and difficult to identify. Fortunately the door was open.

"Is it all right if we go for a walk in the garden?" I asked.

Mrs. Geyer smiled. "I'm afraid you'll find it difficult."

Tsafendas had been seriously ill the previous year, she told me. Pretty close to the wire. His condition now . . . well, I'd see for myself soon. He had very few visitors and nobody could get through to him. His hearing was poor. Not long ago a television crew had come to see him. Was I connected with television? Was there any information I needed?

"I just want to see him. To keep him company."

Matron Geyer promised to bring me a cup of tea.

"He cries a lot, sometimes," she added. "When they show him photos he cries like anything."

Once again I felt nervous, wound up, seized by doubt about my presence here. For this I blamed the yucca. And that smell. I was an intruder; nothing more.

When Demitrios was brought into the room a few moments later, this feeling left me as rapidly as it had come. One of the sturdy nurses pushed a table to one side, rolled a chair on little wheels toward me, and then, in a loud voice, invited us both to sit down.

What a fine head of snow-white hair!

Demitrios's head was tilted to one side. He glanced at me as if from an angle; his gaze was mild, his manner perplexed. It was midday. Perhaps he had just eaten and was ready for a nap.

I shouted at him, in English, "Pleased to meet you."

He was wearing a light-blue T-shirt, with l-o-n-d-o-n printed across it. He was dressed below in a pair of jogging pants, bright green in color, with white stripes running down the sides of the legs. His stomach showed through the gap between his shirt and trousers. His feet were thrust into narrow, ill-fitting, down-at-the-heel slippers.

Matron Geyer returned with a Coca-Cola. She apologized to me for not bringing the tea she had promised; there was none to be had. Demitrios followed her movements as she put the glass down on the side table. He was not allowed to have sweet drinks, she told me. He was overweight and his heart was not strong.

As soon as she left he whispered to me: "You know what they always say. It's the environment. That's what we've discovered. The environment . . ." He made a sweeping gesture with his right arm. "And what it makes of everyone. Anyone you like, in the whole world, the whole world . . ."

His pronunciation of English struck me as odd; I had not imagined that it would sound like this. The intonation was old-fashioned; he had an archaically *middle-class* accent that took me back to my childhood. I might almost have been listening—had I closed my eyes—to one of the adults I used to hear in those days. Or to a good-natured fatty from one of the British children's books I used to read. Or from one of the long-forgotten prewar weekly comics, *The Gem, The Magnet,* something of that sort.

His hand moved compulsively to the cool drink. He leaned toward me. "Do you mind?"

I offered him the glass. He emptied it in one long gulp. He gave a hiccup.

"By the way," he asked, "where do you live? Hopetown? Rustenberg?"

"Holland," I shouted shamelessly in his ear. "Ollandia!"

But it didn't get through to him.

"Thank you very, very much," he replied.

Evidently Demitrios assumed that I had come to listen to him, and without further ado or encouragement he launched into a stream of consciousness or free association, as if sharing recollections with an old acquaintance.

"I've always done whatever I wished. The northern seas, during the war, mountains of stone and ice. It was frightful. I went past the Isle of Stromboli with a ship. The volcano, a live volcano, a brilliant sight."

"And the Isle of Crete?" I shouted back at him.

"Ach, I was there, too. It was very old, dilapidated. But I liked the technology of Turkey. Very good dentistry, too. Solid gold. They make bridges that last forever."

He was rubbing his right hand over his left arm, which rested on his upper leg. He was lame on the left side, I thought. He spoke with a certain sluggishness, which suggested that the movement of his tongue was impaired too.

"The speed of life in the United States of America is

terrific. And the noise! Because of mass production, do you see?" he said enthusiastically. And a moment later: "One thing we have here in Africa, we have time to think, lots of time. We realize now that the environment is stronger than anything. We've got to give Darwin the credit. Darwin's *Evolution of the Species* was an exceptional contribution.

"Look at the motorcar," he went on. "One day they'll be driving big black cars just on sunlight. From the sun's rays they'll drive at seventy-five miles an hour."

Demitrios laughed. Then he sighed. I remained looking at him attentively. Because of his deafness I guessed that he would draw as much from my gaze as from any words that might get through to him. I was surprised by the absence of suspicion in his manner, also by his plainly wanting to reward or oblige me for having come to see him. We sat close together, myself and a man whom I had known for so long from papers only, whose appearance and manner I had drawn from the archives and filled out from my imagination. Now here he was; and here I was, next to him. I felt that the picture I had formed of him over the years had not, after all, been very far from the reality. Or at any rate, it was inaccurate in one regard only: he was more agreeable than I had expected. He could almost have been my father. The two men were the same age: both had been born in 1918. Unwillingly I found myself comparing them. They were both eldest sons who had left home early. Both had become emigrants—wanderers, in fact. Both were deeply dissatisfied, two dreamers who longed to be men of action. But thereafter the comparison went awry. It was out of the differences between them that I had constructed my image of Tsafendas.

From his earliest days Demitrios must have been far more desperate. Must have felt himself incomparably less cherished.

My thoughts had wandered, and Demitrios knew it. He began to speak telegraphically once again, in short sentences, some of them consisting of hardly more than a single word, with a heavy emphasis on the consonants.

"We had this huge place in Lourenço Marques, this meeting place for Greeks. They came there to speak to each other in High Greek. Ah, Crete. My father was born in Crete, during the Turkish Ottoman empire. The Turks used to rule over most of the islands in those days. My father was a special drinker of Turkish coffee. He taught me how to boil it . . . He used to sing in Turkish. He smoked Greek cigarettes, Venizelos brand . . ."

Occasionally he would let his head drop tiredly, then raise it again. He embarked on a long monologue in the course of which he spoke of the harbors of Herakleion, Chania, Piraeus, Lourenço Marques. Then, without any link between one subject and the next, he was talking of Greek architecture. And that led him back to the Greek community in Lourenço Marques.

"I want to make a mausoleum there, with the assistance of the people who built the big buildings. They were Greeks, all of them. The Acropolis, the department store. The St. George. Big. Out of nothing. The man who built the Acropolis had rickshaw boys working for him"—he laughed briefly at the memory—"terribly slowly, brick by brick. And underneath, all shops. They made a *city* out of Lourenço Marques.

"Those Greeks were very conservative. My biological mother wanted me to go further with Greek history. She influenced me. She was a very cosmopolitan woman. She spoke French quite well. I wish I could see her now. They lived, the last time I saw them, in Proclamation Hill, Pretoria. And the City Tearoom, Quagga Road."

He yawned. I waited. When he resumed he again confused his natural mother with Marika, his stepmother. It was plain to me that they had not merged with each other in his mind after all these years. The distinction between them had remained clear. But he had exchanged their identities and names. Just as I, I found myself thinking, had always believed the wound inflicted on him in Natal to have been on his left arm. But it was his right arm that bore the scar. Elsewhere his skin was fine in texture, almost hairless, surprisingly smooth for a man of eighty.

"That wound," he said thoughtfully. "I no longer remember exactly what happened. I was stabbed in Port Shepstone. What a job it was to sew it up! They operated to join the tendons. They wanted to give me an anesthetic. I refused . . . I went to Stuttafords to have a cup of tea, tea with toast. I'll never forget the rickshaws in Durban. Do you still remember the rickshaws in Durban?"

•

Matron Geyer put her head around the corner. Was everything all right? Yes, fine. Demitrios and I sat and smiled at each other, the old man still holding forth, I responding with nods.

"We Greeks were rivals against the Orientals. Very strong rivals. They brought me up very strict against the Orientals, the Arabs especially . . . I was taken out of the French mission school. I was learning the black language there, Shangaan. It was a big mistake. They should have left me but they sent me to a Catholic Portuguese school. And from there they took me out again and sent me to school in Middelburg, in the Transvaal. I had difficulty because of Afrikaans in one class and English in the other. I didn't know Afrikaans. But I kept on, I persisted. I had no choice because my parents were so strict.

"I had a big tooth pulled out there by a dentist called de Villiers. That tooth made history. He couldn't yank it out. I was sitting in the hall with all the other children and they were laughing. He got angry and chased them out of the room. It was *big*, the root. All night I was losing blood on my pillow. That was in Nelson House, the school hostel. When I visited London the first thing I wanted to visit was Nelson's *Victory* ship. And when I went there I signed my name in the book. The guard said: 'Put your address there, sign your name . . .' "

He told the story with evident satisfaction, proud that the man had asked him for his signature. If he had been somewhat subdued initially, he was now animated, alert, carried away by his words. He spoke about his childhood days in

Alexandria and the house of his grandmother Tsafandakis. He had long had in his possession a photograph of himself as a little boy, in Arab garb.

"I kept it. I put it in an envelope when I was in Pretoria Central prison. Potgieter, he destroyed it. It disappeared there. I used to keep it, but Potgieter, the chief warder, destroyed it, also my birth certificate. I had all that. I knew it was historic. But Potgieter was against me, he tore everything up. It would make history, but that stupid Potgieter . . ."

He trailed off, agitatedly, weeping. He repeatedly complained about that incident.

"Potgieter was *furious* against anything that belonged to me. But his helper was very good to me. I'd like to see him. He sympathized with me and protected me whenever possible, when I was beaten on the skull. Blood used to come in! He was also an Afrikaner, but different . . .

"Completely different, very good-natured," he repeated.

A little later, clearly referring still to the prison in Pretoria, he said: "I'd like to go back there, where I used to live in that building. It's been transformed into a holy place now. A holy place. You must find out. You must inquire."

Outside, a light breeze had begun to blow over the lawns of Sterkfontein. I had spent hours in Demitrios's presence. His recollections were fragmented in a manner that was peculiarly his own. The Greek African storyteller.

Scrabbling through the dislocations of time, confined within his defective hearing, he picked up tiny moments of his memories, like bits of stone, and let them drop. The longer I listened, however, the more I began to suspect that his manner of jumping from topic to topic was also a way of testing me, perhaps to find out how much I knew of his history. Was he then merely playing games? No, not always, and not with any definite aim, but still—Demitrios gave the impression of being someone who was used to improvising with whatever he retained of his past. As if he had often been compelled to sort through it. Or as if the film of his existence consisted of hundreds of rushes that still had to be edited. So he was free to put them together differently each time.

At one point he began to sing English songs from fifty years ago—for old times' sake, he said, the spit flying out of the corner of his mouth. He had become positively elated. Among the songs was "A Bicycle Built for Two." Drawing deep breaths he also burst into "Onward, Christian soldiers/ Marching as to war/With the cross of Jesus/Going on before . . ."

Weeks later the smell of that visit was still with me. It was the smell of old, unwashed men. The rotten sweetness of uncared-for teeth and unwashed armpits, mixed with the odor of half-digested food rising from the bowels and through the pores of the skin. Demitrios was a neglected creature. That was the truth. Matron Geyer was not to be blamed. There was nothing she could do about it. The hospital was hopelessly understaffed.

Just before I left he asked, "Are you an enthusiast of flying?"

The question was wonderfully dated. It belonged, I thought, to an era of golfing caps and plus fours on English greens: it was a question that polite young men might have asked each other on first getting acquainted, in 1928, say, when you could not take for granted the prospect of traveling by air. Or, for that matter, when you did not know if your acquaintances were regular listeners to that other newfangled contraption, the wireless.

As I got up to go he made me promise to return the next day.

Back in the hotel in Krugersdorp. The Afrikaner cowboys and cowgirls were still hanging around in the bar. Weak with hunger, I went to the dining room. I was the only guest, waited on by a girl who from time to time fiddled with the hem of her miniskirt. Music came incessantly out of the speakers on the walls, as numbing as ever. The walls, the ceiling, and the carpet in the room were green; so were the tablecloths. But not any old green: this was a dark, alpine-hat color, with here and there, by way of contrast, a hint of somber red. I was eating in a green-red womb, under a sign of romance, Transvaal-style. By which I mean the two exaggeratedly blue and purple paintings, landscapes both, hung on the walls. One showed a gilded ship daintily stranded on rocks, the other a blood-curdling sunset seen through a thornbush, while two bucks and a rhino drank at a nearby pool.

My thoughts were still in Sterkfontein. The meeting had left me feeling dizzy. I had come assuming that I would meet an extinguished human being. Someone whose illness could only have been exacerbated by three decades of imprisonment and maltreatment. A man whom witnesses had described after the attack, almost without exception, in wholly unsympathetic terms: a pig, a liar, a nutcase. Surely after his "release," his transfer to an asylum, I would find him infantile, deaf, manifestly crazy.

What I had found, instead, was a charming chatterbox. A survivor from the detritus of South African history.

Why was he still confined in the wretched institution in which I had found him? Between 1942 and 1963 alone—his period abroad—he had been arrested five times, deported five times, twice incarcerated for long periods, and eight times refused entry into South Africa. During the fifties and sixties he had regarded himself as a kind of pilgrim, that much was clear. A man with a mission, even if he could never have said exactly where his Mecca lay. Now that everything was long behind him, he remained one of the few among the huge band of exiles who had never been able to come home again, either literally or metaphorically.

Most people know how to give their past a form that seems plausible to themselves and others. We tell and retell a chronologically ordered story and seldom lose the knack of giving to particular incidents within that story—the successive events of childhood, physical or spiritual traumas, the loss of parents or loved ones—more emphasis than others. We have put them in line, so to speak. Demitrios had never managed it. There was no such line in his consciousness. He was incapable of arranging his past, or even of separating it from the present. The connections he made were not chronological but mythical. Almost any incident of his life could be enlarged or colored as he wished, as if he looked at himself through a strange lens that dissociated him from the every-dayness of his psyche. In a sense he had acquired the gift of a sophisticated storyteller: he looked on time as an ever-changing substance or as nothing more than a hypothesis that might be abandoned here or there, depending on the effect, or that was controlled by a higher allegorical meaning. But for Demitrios this habit must have often brought him pain rather than pleasure; must have been a source of torment.

That afternoon, sitting next to an old man comprehensively saying his piece (and willingly, too, as if he might never have another chance to do it), I had felt myself endowed with unusual perspicacity. No doubt his stories sounded like concoctions to those who knew little or nothing of his background. For him, all he had ever been, all he could ever speak of, was secluded within a domain of glass, viewable only through a lens scored by sharp cracks and flaws.

In the green dining room of that hotel in Krugersdorp I asked myself if I knew of a better way of trying to apprehend the history of his country.

"Please let's go somewhere," he greeted me the next morning. "I don't know where I am. Everything looks so strange to me. Can I go into the sunshine? Obtain some sunshine?"

The hefty nurse I had seen yesterday walked past.

"*Haai*, Mr. Tsafendas." He hit Demitrios good-humoredly on the back and stretched out his dark hand in an African-style greeting, taking the patient's hand by the palm and then by the thumb.

"Ah, the strong man," Demitrios answered, saying the last

words as if they were a name rather than a description. Then, to me: "He's a really good chap. A very virtuous man. But strong."

We were sitting in the same room as before. Today Demitrios was wearing a striped polo shirt with white buttons. STERK-FONTEIN HOSPITAL 12B had been written with a felt-tip pen in crooked letters across it. He spoke more clearly than he had previously and was more emotionally affected by what he was saying. The stories came out as if he had spent far too long in solitude. But as for the topics they touched on, they were what they had always been.

"My biological mother was a strong woman. Not very big but well-proportioned—an athletic figure. Her face was full of smallpox holes. She had a sister. I love her sister. I'm in love with her. Very delicate and amusing. But she married this Greek wrestler, a champion from the United States. He was muscle-bound. They did not match. She got sick, she nearly died. She was so delicate and angelic. I loved her, till today. But this man . . . He was cheated into coming to Africa by his relations. He owned a biscuit bakery, he specialized in pastry and some kinds of sweets and chocolates. It was a mistake this aunt of mine made, marrying that wrestler."

Then, looking around for the attendant, "And where's the strong man? Where is he?"

He rubbed his pant leg, with some difficulty lifting his paralyzed left leg over his right knee.

"He's very virtuous. Healthy, too, the strong man. But where is he? I'm searching for my false teeth . . . Oh *ja,* they're in the washroom."

The strong man returned with a plate of food: rice, spinach, beef cut into small pieces. While I held the plate for him, Demitrios fed himself with a plastic hospital spoon. He stuffed the food into his mouth but chewed each mouthful thoroughly. Eventually, working earnestly and systematically, he succeeded in emptying the plate. With the rim of his spoon he gathered the remaining grains of rice. Some of them spilled while he was eating, so I brushed them off his lap and shook them off his shirt.

After lunch his thoughts veered off on another tack. "I wanted to have strong children. So I restrained myself from women. I kept myself chaste. No smoking, nothing. Working all the time. No whiskey drinking. Milk shakes I drink, Coca-Cola and Pepsi-Cola. In Egypt we have a special drink from sugarcane, I don't remember what they call it. And pineapples. Watermelon. Sweet melon."

He fell silent.

I wrote on the pad: WAS THERE A WOMAN IN YOUR LIFE?

He read the question slowly, as if spelling it out letter by letter. It did not seem to dismay him. On the contrary, he set about answering it like a conscientious autobiographer, from the very beginning.

"The first woman in my life, I was young, I was underage. She was Portuguese and I used to go with her. She said to me, 'What do you like? Do you want to copulate or do you want me to suck you off?' I said to her, 'I want to copulate. I want to push.' I was very small . . ."

He laughed, relieved and amused at the memory. "I remember she was living in a house and next door was Gregoris. He was the Greek making ice cream, he used to sell ice cream to the city. I used to go and speak to Gregoris, then I met this woman."

"And in Cape Town?" I asked.

"No, I did not know any woman in Cape Town. In Istanbul, yes, I had a girlfriend in Turkey. She was very intelligent. She got me the job in the college as a professor of English. She spoke to the authorities. And in Athens, one of the Greek girls in my church loved me. But she died. A great love. And in Pretoria I went to the social workers' meetings and there was a Dutch girl there, very beautiful. But the preacher of the Gospel, he kept her away from me, he wanted her to himself . . . In America, too, there was a beautiful girl, an American, and in Germany one of the workers I liked . . . But I could not compete.

"My biological mother used to call me Mimis. She liked me, but I was in love with her sister, Annie. The one with the wrestler . . . Can you remember Marlene Dietrich?"

I nodded.

"Aha!" he laughed. He began to sing, "Falling in love again, what am I to do? Falling in love again." The next half hour went by with more songs ("Deep Purple," "Jeepers Creepers," "I Can't Give You Anything but Love, Baby") and a fond listing of the names of bygone film stars: Charlie Chaplin, Syd Chaplin, William Boyd, Douglas Fairbanks, Lana Turner. Buster Keaton remained his favorite, however, together with Dietrich. *"Bei mir bist du schön, bei mir bist du schön und wunderbar . . ."*

Snatches of Greek, Italian, and Portuguese songs followed. Of the Greek song he said, "That one was very romantic."

•

"Good morning." It was one of the doctors, Dr. Hamukoma, who had been drawn to the room by our singing. She tugged gently at the shoulder of Demitrios's shirt. "How are you?"

"Adventures, adventures, all over the world," Demitrios replied. "Germany. The ships' bunkers on the river. Frankfurt am Main."

Dr. Hamukoma looked at me. She could not understand a word he was saying.

"Ships' bunkers. *Schiffsbunker,* with concrete walls, one meter sixty thick. I sat outside, to watch, in a little field. There were children playing. German children. They give me *Haselnüße,* hazelnuts, the small children. They pick them from the trees and give them to me. They were so kind . . . I didn't have any chocolate to pay them back."

The doctor said to me: "He's quite sweet."

She was a slender black woman, exceptionally attractive. Why was it just then that Demitrios had to go right off the edge?

"Now I want to give them something. I want to go back to the *Schiffsbunker,*" he said, starting to sob. "I want to thank those children. They were very good to me, these girls, the small, little girls."

And still sobbing: "'*Bei mir bist du schön und wunderbar.*'"

Dr. Hamukoma comforted him, holding his arm in both her hands. I wanted to explain to her what he had been talking about, but it was impossible to give a context to his words, since she evidently knew little of his life story.

Demitrios: "'You laugh today, you cry tomorrow.' Do you remember that song too?"

"He badly needs a hearing aid," I said to the doctor. She answered that the money to get him one was simply not available. Recently they had unsuccessfully tried to raise funds to provide one for another patient. The money was just not to be had.

"I want to hear those records again," Demitrios said, after the doctor had left us to go on with her rounds. "I know the rhythm, I just have to pick it up. *Anything* you want to ask me, ask me. I will tell you. I have a very good memory."

That was not exactly what I had come for—an interrogation, an investigation.

"I can remember everything," he assured me.

I picked up pencil and paper and wrote, "*Eugenie Livanos.*"

"*Livanos,* 1942. I was working there in the bakery. Down in the machine room. A very big boat. A Greek ship. They had contraband on board. Narcotics. But I had nothing to do with it. The captain was all right. He taught me how to steer the ship. Took me on the bridge—port, starboard, 360 degrees. He protected me. But the crew—very rough. The engine-room crew tried to rape me. They tried to convince me to have sex with them, but I wouldn't. When we got to Canada the immigration authorities took me to *Eugenie Livanos.* 'Do you want to go back on this ship? Do you want to work on this ship again?' I was then in prison. I said, 'No!' So they left without me."

After a silence, and with the air of one passing on an item

of information I might find useful, he added: "A big per-
centage of homosexuals among the Greeks.

"My father was very strict," he went on. "He always *watched*
you, in case . . ." He made masturbatory gestures with his
hand.

"He was an engineer. He sacrificed his life to a perpetual-
motion machine. And I continued in his footsteps. My
brother was also a lathe turner. But my biological mother, she
spoiled my brother. In the morning she gives him eggs, fried
eggs, scrambled eggs. He, not me. He was born with one leg
first, out of my stepmother. Not with the head. She was
screaming all night. It was a breech birth. That's why she is
like that."

His chin sank toward his chest and he stuck out his lower
lip, as if sulking. Then he lifted his head, recalling something
important.

"She made a big mistake in Lourenço Marques when a
Portuguese chemist discovered I had a tapeworm. He gave
me some medicine, an extract, a powerful poison. He said,
'You must bring the species' head. I must study it.' I drink the
extract and the following day it started coming out. I went to
the toilet and half of it was out, two or three meters. But the
chemist had said, 'You must not throw it away. You must
bring it to me. I want to study it.' My stepmother said, 'It's
out, out.' She put it in the toilet."

He mimed the pulling of a toilet chain.

"A big mistake! A very big mistake! Two or three
meters . . . I think it's still alive in the sewers, because it
doesn't die, it's very strong. And the Portuguese chemist was

very angry. He said, 'Why did you throw it away?' But the sewer is still there. I want to study the sewer underneath the old house. I want to go back to the sewer."

He gazed at me with amber-colored eyes. "You must help me." And later, wistfully, after I had taken a picture of him, "I want you to photograph me in front of my house, in front of my property. I want you to help me."

When I got back to my room that afternoon I phoned Johannesburg. After following various false trails I learned that there was a social worker attached to the Greek Orthodox Church who had shown some concern for Demitrios. In the evening I managed to reach her. She must have been more than fifty years old, but she had a surprisingly youthful voice. The ice was soon broken. She was pleasantly surprised to hear that she was not alone in being troubled by Demitrios's fate. Had I noticed how dirty he was? He should really have been moved into a private clinic. But no one was ready to put up the money to make that possible. The community—and there were eighty thousand Greeks in the Transvaal alone— was not interested in him. He was a man under a stigma still; people preferred to let sleeping dogs lie. In Pretoria there were also two half-sisters, stepsisters, but because of the political implications of his case people in the community wanted to have nothing to do with him. Even at Easter nobody from the family went to visit him, though it was the most important festival of the Orthodox Church. She couldn't understand it.

"And the authorities?" I asked.

Well, when Demitrios had almost died six months earlier, she had received a telephone call from the Health Department. Someone high up, she assumed, must have given the word for her to be contacted. She was told that in the event of his death the press should not be informed. No publicity whatever was to be given to the matter. He was to be buried quietly and only then would a brief press statement follow.

She had sat next to his bed for two days, accompanied by an Orthodox priest. He had stubbornly refused to die.

She knew little of his background. He had never spoken to her about his past in South Africa. He was very uncommunicative when she visited him in the institution.

"Who are you?" he would ask her. And: "Why do you come here?"

Still, she did go to see him from time to time. He was such a dear, soft-natured man and so lonely. What she could never bring herself to understand was that he had been able to commit a murder. Someday somebody would have to explain that.

The compassionate social worker was not the only one who found it difficult to imagine how deeply a man like Demitrios would have felt the dilemma of the "baster"—the bastard, the half-blood. How it must have maimed his sense of self-worth and how hopeless he must have been as a result. Nonwhites were generally regarded by whites as dirty, animal-like, untrustworthy, but the half-breed was the worst, precisely because he was so close to whites themselves.

"You like chocolate?" The question had been flung at me seven years earlier by a crowd of young coloreds at a suburban Cape Town station, as I emerged from the train with a young colored woman. She took my arm and walked on resolutely. I did not dare to look back at the people taunting me. The anger, the mixture of scorn and envy in their voices, the surprise and derision were plain. What they were holding me responsible for was also evident.

Now that overt racial prejudice is considered virtually antique in much of the world, or is at least vociferously repudiated, there is a danger that the history of all those of mixed race in South Africa will be suppressed, rendered incomprehensible. Inwardly we white north Europeans are choosing to forget the contours of our craziness, the overwhelming ugliness of our fear of bastardy. Simply, the colored was defined by what he was *not*. Not white and not black. Even the "native peoples" were regarded as preferable to the half-blood; they were at least "pure"; to them, fragmentary notions of the "noble savage" still clung. But the coloreds were neither noble nor savage. Far from it. They were the evidence-become-flesh of white depravity and deceit, and hence every colored person could be seen as a wandering object of shame. The sacred borders between species had been transgressed and this was the result.

Throughout his life Demitrios claimed that somewhere in southern Africa there was a woman waiting for him, the love of his youth. Even as a figment of his imagination, however, this ideal figure threatened to produce for him dark-skinned progeny who would bring to light the concealed hereditary stigma of his bad blood. He could cross the line, go over, play white, though he always carried within him the self-estrangement of his dark conscience. Or he could take on the role of the shamed and vengeful colored. He could destroy the chief of the white tribe, which, once his wanderings through Europe had miserably ended, is what he did. With or without the help of the tapeworm inside him, he cut off the creature's head.

A few hours after the murder Verwoerd's wife was heard to comfort herself with the words, "God does not make mistakes."

But Demitrios needed no command from heaven to do what he did. His deed was the direct consequence of sublunary traumas. The tribal sentiments of the Afrikaner were derived in large measure from some of the same sentiments that Tsafendas harbored: a longing to feel truly at home, a search for acknowledgment, a conviction that he had spent too long wandering in the wilderness. The Afrikaner was ready to maintain his homeland through violence, the violence of the state, if need be. His preoccupation with racial purity and unsoiled blood was central to that aim.

Which of the two, then, was more truly crazy: Verwoerd or Tsafendas?

It was hardly possible to exaggerate the importance of what Demitrios had done, I reflected in my room in the Krugersdorp hotel. The attack on Verwoerd was a proclamation of the end of the doctrine of apartheid, of the idiotic dread of "racial mixing." It presaged the hesitant beginning of integration. Of a mixed-up living together—the very idea that had horrified so many generations of white South Africans. Of the birth of the "rainbow nation" that, in a bout of overexcitement and child-like honesty, Demitrios had called for in 1964.

I had never been able to find words for the feelings that overwhelmed me on the afternoon of the attack. Retrospectively, it now seemed that the power of madness had at that moment shown itself equal to the madness of power, as if nature itself had finally righted the balance between the two.

On Friday, 27 March, I paid my last visit to Demitrios. I took with me a small Greek stringed instrument, a *baglamá,* in the hope of diverting him. This time Ward 12B was not prepared for my arrival. During my previous visit I had merely said that I might be returning, and no one had made any objection.

On this Friday hardly any of the staff were in attendance. The strong man led me to a hall where Demitrios sat dozing in the middle of a group of patients. The attendant left us, locking the door behind him. I found myself in a long, narrow space, an enclosed porch with a wall of rough brick at one end and rusty-framed metal windows at the other. Among the twenty-odd patients it was difficult at first for me to pick out the nurse. She sat bent over a magazine and made no acknowledgment of my arrival. Her sphere of action appeared to be confined to the corner of the room next to the TV, which was turned up loud and burst out with great clamor every now and again. The noise was deafening, the smell in the room fetid and penetrating.

Watched by the others, I moved a chair next to Demitrios. The man to his left shouted something I could not understand though it was clearly addressed to me. He was a muscular fellow in a striped robe. Almost everyone wore a similar blue-striped dressing gown, though many simply had it slung over their shoulders or tied by the arms around their waists. Demitrios was wearing his robe backward. It made him look absurd. Next to him sat a man apparently incapable of speech. While I waited I could do little more than look about me quietly. Conversation was impossible here.

Demitrios woke slowly. We waved to each other; then he made another gesture of complicity, a scraping movement of his thumb against his cheek, which I alone, having spent some time in Greece, could decipher.

He had no slippers on his feet. His right leg was stretched out in front of him. Around the big toe was a gauze bandage, through which some dried blood showed. The tape holding the bandage in place was loose, and some of it had curled itself under his chair.

Facing us sat a young man. On his head was an open wound and a few tufts of hair.

"He's an epileptic," Demitrios said, almost inaudibly, and made a small circular movement of his hand—another Greek gesture, indicating that the patient was in a bad way. The man sat with his chair tilted dangerously forward.

When the strong man with the keys returned, I asked him if Mr. Tsafendas could be brought into a room next door. Reluctantly, he agreed. We had to lift Demitrios into a wheelchair. He was disconcertingly heavy. The person sitting closest to him had to be unceremoniously moved out of the way. I saw bits of food lying on the linoleum and a half-dried patch of damp. Then each of us took Demitrios by an armpit and, with difficulty, decanted him into his vehicle.

In the big room next to the kitchen he recovered his breath.

"Have you got any chocolate?"

Alas, no.

He mumbled a few words about the chocolate in Middelburg. Once again I was struck by his English. It was an English that was hardly spoken anymore, to which he gave a dragging intonation, a certain emphasis on particular syllables that could only have come from the Greek.

I showed him the *baglamá* and strummed a little tune on it.

"Very interesting instrument," Demitrios said. "Small in size. Delicate sound. I would have liked to have been able to play it myself. Or the piano accordion. The organ. Before that I was interested in the bugle. That was in Middelburg."

Then, in a whisper, "Play some more."

The *baglamá* has a piercing but attractive sound; I was glad he was able to hear it.

"Do you play the violin, too? The saxophone? That's what I'd really like to do."

The next question came out of the blue. He asked me who the president of South Africa was now.

On my little pad I wrote the name "Mandela" and showed it to him.

"Nelson Mandela . . . ? I would like to speak to him. He's a very strong man."

When I made a few movements with my fists, like a boxer, Demitrios laughed out loud. From the hall behind us a harsh screaming suddenly broke out. If a stone could screech, it would make a noise like that. Then came the sounds of crashing crockery and another loud voice trying to restore order.

Demitrios had fallen silent. If I was ever going to ask the question, this had to be the moment. "Do you remember Verwoerd?" I scrawled on my pad with suddenly awkward fingers. I handed it to him.

"I didn't know Hendrik Verwoerd personally." Demitrios sighed. He thought for a moment. "I had never spoken to him before . . ."

The racket in the hall broke out briefly once more. I heard the footsteps of Demitrios's strong man and the unlocking of the door that led to the closed section of the ward.

Demitrios moved uneasily in his wheelchair.

"I do regret . . . ," he stammered. "I *do* regret . . . ," he said again and yet again, for the third time. "I *regret* . . ." He took the paper and pencil out of my hand.

When he returned the pad to me I saw that he had written four words in untidy block letters.

I REGRET WHAT HAPPENED.

He began to cry. I took both his shoulders in my hands and shouted as loudly as I could, "Never mind. Other times. Not your fault."

"A whole other time," he sobbed. "I am not that kind of

person. It was something that happened. It was not in my nature. Besides, I was sick."

His striped robe had fallen from his chest. Poor Mimis. He placed the blame on the doctors. It was their fault. They should have operated on him. Why hadn't they done it? He pointed to his stomach. Why hadn't they removed the creature in there? Either they could not or they would not do it.

"It will not die. I'm helpless against this Dragon-Tapeworm. I cannot do anything. But they won't investigate. Too difficult and very complicated. At night when I sleep I see orgies. All imagination. Visions."

Then he told me that while he'd been working in parliament, he had heard from a woman member of the house that Verwoerd was not an upright human being. It was one of the things, he wanted me to know, that had set him thinking of what had to be done. "She came to me—I found out later she was a member of the United Party—and she said, 'Hendrik Verwoerd is a very immoral person.' You see? When she told me that I went down . . . and that's how it started. *She* stirred me. She made me angry."

Again he began to weep, then made an effort to compose himself. "I went down to the shopping center on the Herengracht and bought a knife. I went inside and I said, 'Give me a knife.' The woman gave me a little knife. I said, 'It's too small. Give me a bigger knife.'"

When he had fallen silent I wrote a few more words on the pad. "'Like a real Cretan,'" Demitrios read slowly. "Yeh," he said calmly. "Nature, hereditary nature.

"It's nature," he said again, with an air of finality. "Human nature."

When we said good-bye he pulled me close to him, embracing me with one of his arms, and pressed, between sobs, a fatherly kiss on my cheek and forehead.

The strong man was waiting to see me off.

Early in October 1999, at the beginning of the South African spring, Demitrios became ill and was transferred to a ward in which his physical ailments could be treated. He was suffering, not for the first time, from pneumonia, a condition aggravated by chronic heart disease. After a few days, on Thursday, 7 October, the eighty-one-year-old patient finally succumbed.

That he had survived for so long attests in itself to his resilience. At four o'clock that afternoon the superintendent of the Krugersdorp hospital phoned the Orthodox church in Pretoria and spoke to the lady from the Greek welfare organization whom I had contacted during my last visit. The family had to be informed and arrangements made. Everything, the welfare worker was given to understand, should be done with the utmost discretion. As little publicity as possible was to attend the occasion.

In fact, the media had got wind of the event almost immediately. The news of Tsafendas's death was broadcast on national television within hours and was a lead item in the evening's news services. The first reports said that he would receive a pauper's burial, since he had no immediate family to pay the expenses involved.

Strictly speaking, this was inaccurate. Two of Demitrios's half-sisters had lately been living in Pretoria; at the time of his death they were reported to be in Greece. It was not clear whether they were merely visiting the country or were now residing there. It made no difference. For decades the two aged women had had nothing to do with their wayward brother.

By Friday the welfare worker—acting as spokeswoman for the Hellenic Orthodox Ladies' Association (HOLA)—had consulted with Archbishop Ionannis of Pretoria. Together they agreed that the Orthodox Church would assume responsibility for the funeral. In coming to this decision they took into account, among other things, the signs of piety Demitrios had displayed in his later years. HOLA would see that a coffin was ordered and would make arrangements for the service. It was scheduled for the following Monday at Aghios Andreas church in Krugersdorp, which served the small but well-to-do Orthodox community on the east Rand. Its priest—Demitrios Vergitsis—was willing to take on the duty, whatever risks might be involved.

That evening, probably acting under pressure of the publicity being given to the event, Archbishop Ionannis decided that the funeral should be moved up to the very next day. The authorities insisted that a strong security presence be in place throughout.

•

Saturday morning, 9 October, a bright spring day, saw a hand-ful of mourners converging on the church in Krugersdorp. They were outnumbered by members of the press corps, who were in turn outnumbered by plainclothes and uni-formed members of the South African police, the latter accompanied by several large, nervous search dogs.

Among those who had come to pay their respects were Patrick and Louise O'Ryan, the couple Demitrios had stayed with in Lansdowne, Cape Town, in 1966, who had remained in touch with him, official discouragement notwithstanding, through all his years in prison and asylum. They had flown in on a few hours' notice. Also present were Aron Mabe, a member of the Pan-Africanist Congress, and Gagi Mohane, a member of the African National Congress. They were there in their private capacities, however. To a journalist taking notes, one of them said, "We are burying a human being whom we believe to have been a hero." Apart from the police, no official representatives from the government or the opposition parties attended the service.

The two Tsafandakis sisters had either been unable or unwilling to have flowers sent in their name. Shortly before the service began, a large wreath of white lilies arrived—the only floral tribute received—and was carried into the church. It had been sent by Liza Key, a filmmaker who had befriended Demitrios in the course of making a television documentary on his life. She had also seen to it that a plaque would be placed on the coffin by one of the reporters, a friend of hers who worked for the Johannesburg *Sunday Inde-pendent*. It read: *Dimitri Tsafendas 1918–1999: Displaced Per-son, Sailor, Christian, Communist, Liberation Fighter, Political Prisoner, Hero: Remembered By His Friends.*

Disturbed perhaps by the arrival of the plaque or by the wreath of lilies, the police dogs went into a sudden paroxysm of barking and pulling at their leads. After some uproar the police had the building cleared. While the priest, the congre-gation, and the attendant reporters waited on the pavement, the search dogs did what they were trained to do. Nothing was found. The incident would have amused Demitrios greatly, I suspect. No doubt a younger Tsafendas would also have been gratified by the words on the plaque: Liberation Fighter, Sailor, Hero . . . Perhaps only "Professor of English" was missing.

Once the police had given the all clear, Father Vergitsis pro-ceeded with the service. He spoke of "pastures where there will be neither sorrow nor mourning. Nor will there be judg-ment."

Soon after midday the group of mourners straggled along a pathway through the cemetery adjacent to the grounds of Sterkfontein Hospital. The grave had been dug in a corner used for interring the poorest of the poor: vagrants and those without next of kin. Mrs. O'Ryan wept quietly, her husband by her side. The last rituals were performed. With a symbolic gesture peculiar to the Orthodox Church, the priest poured oil over the casket—a reenactment of the anointing that welcomes a newcomer (whether infant or adult) to the faith. Then the coffin was lowered, the pit was filled in, the mourners went their separate ways.

Mimis's burial place has remained unmarked. No tombstone has been erected. No sign identifies the spot. It has simply disappeared among the mounds, rubble, and tangled grass of the immediate vicinity.

NOTES

The life of Demitrios Tsafendas has never been the subject of a book. So a few words on my rendering of his history seem to be called for.

Virtually all the information about him presented here is drawn from primary sources. A difficult problem arose once I had set about trying to reconstruct the course of his life. Anyone who goes through an archive is bound to find in it papers that seem to grow in significance even as a painful, contradictory sense of their limitations becomes more and more apparent. I could have chosen to present Demitrios's life as the sources invited, as a collection of shards. But the result would hardly have been readable, nor would it have done justice to his predicament. In some instances, therefore, I have taken my cue from the restoration of archaeological finds.

Not long ago it was the practice to present the fragments revealed in a dig in the most naturalistic manner possible. Earlier still a contrary principle of "originality" was followed: curators attempted to bring order to the remains of the past and make their original form apparent to the onlooker, often by adding some neutral filler. Speculative additions to the material, however, were precluded. In both cases the aim was to show something that no longer existed; in both cases a measure of artifice had to be used.

The amount of material that confronted me was overwhelming. In the State Archives in Pretoria alone, I came on twelve large cartons packed with documents gathered by the security police and the Ministry of Justice (some of which have since disappeared). They had been assembled as evidence in the event of a full trial, which never took place. In the time and space available I struggled to arrange what I had come across in the style of "neutral restoration" described above.

The events of Demitrios's life, the places he visited, the people he met, and the conversations he had are either factually accurate or inferred from other episodes and from my conversations with the man himself. Inferences of this kind are indicated in the text by a kind of deliberate hesitation (e.g., "who, if anyone, might have been pulling strings behind the scenes" on page 80) or presented unambiguously as a form of scene painting (e.g., "he was joyfully applauded and thrown onto the sandy beach" on page 69).

All that said, it would clearly be false for me to claim that my impression of Demitrios's selfhood and inner consciousness was based exclusively on facts that could be established retrospectively. His innermost life—that which he *felt*—had to be grasped intuitively. A transaction can be verified. A dilemma, his dilemma, is much harder to delineate. To do that I had to rely on instinct, an intuitive understanding of his personality and the things that affected him. Needless to say, the endeavor was made all the more compelling for me by our having struck up an acquaintance.

It was my conviction—one sustained over the last decade by meetings I have had and observations I have made—that by means of Demitrios's story I would be able to render something of the South African trauma. In that sense my book is a cautious attempt to achieve an anamnesis—a bringing back to memory of that which has been forgotten. No matter how immodest the effort may appear to be, I wanted to present in bold outline my perception of his, and the country's, turmoil during the tragic years of apartheid. Still, to try to recall the history of someone's illness is not the same thing as rendering a diagnosis.

....

A full apparatus of notes would imply that I was aiming for quasi-scientific objectivity. That was never my ambition. Nevertheless I trust that the reader will find the notes and references below illuminating.

pages 1–5 On 11 February 1955 . . . the knife in his right hand: This dramatization of Demitrios's stay in Hamburg's General Hospital is drawn from detailed reports written irregularly in a journal describing the course of the patient's illness. The notes were subsequently copied by the Ochsenzoll Clinic and, at his request, were sent to Dr. I. Sakinofsky of Groote Schuur Hospital in Cape Town (see p. 117). I found them in the State Archives in Pretoria in March 1998. The faded brown suit in which I dress Demitrios on his discharge from the hospital is derived from a line by the Alexandrian poet K. P. Kaváfis, a fellow townsman of his between 1919 and 1925.

page 7 the journalist Gordon Winter: Those who wish to know more of this man, an unscrupulous servant of the apartheid regime and a former golfing partner of B. J. Vorster, the South African prime minister from 1966 to 1978, can study the self-portrait he presents in his book.

pages 9 ff. Hendrik Frensch Verwoerd: It is not my ambition to give a full account of his life; all I have done is mention (possibly to caricatural effect) a few salient facts that Demitrios himself would have known. See also *Dr. Hendrik Frensch Verwoerd,* by G. D. Scholtz (Johannesburg, 1974), a hagiography of over 600 pages, and H. O. Terblanche, "Hollandse Afkoms van Verwoerd," *Zuid-Afrika,* August 1998.

page 11 "basters"—half-castes: The first time Demitrios was officially categorized in these terms was in a letter from the South African consul general in Lourenço Marques to the headquarters of the South African police in Marshall Square, Johannesburg, on 29 June 1937: "The above-named is a half-caste . . . employed in Lourenço Marques Kiosk about a year ago, but dismissed owing to his communistic leanings."

page 13 Emigration was an experience I, too, had undergone: At the end of the Second World War, a third of the population of the Netherlands was ready to consider emigration. Between 1946 and 1954, before my own family's departure, more than 200,000 Netherlanders actually emigrated. Of these, about a tenth went directly to South Africa. The new South Africans were subsidized by a bonus of 5,000 guilders per immigrant—in effect a kind of bribe or "relocation allowance." In 1955 a special committee was set up for the overseas celebration of St. Nicholas's Day. A different Dutch habit—the riding of bicycles—was abandoned in South Africa: their use was confined in that country to "kaffirs and servants," according to Du Plessis, *Nederlandse Emigrasie naar Suid-Afrika* (Pretoria, 1956).

page 15 How many South Africans were forced out of their cities during the fifties and sixties?: The first large-scale displacement of population, from Sophiatown in Johannesburg in February 1955, fell directly under Verwoerd's ministerial responsibility. Throughout the operation he was kept informed in his office by the police via express telegraph. The police reported that the black population left their homes in a joyful spirit: "Many of the Bantus in the street appear to be in picnic mood."

page 34 Erotokritas: Poiema Erotikon Legomenon Erotikritos (Vincenzo Kornarou, Venice, 1713) is the national epic of Crete, which Katerina would without doubt have known. I have seldom met a Cretan who has been unable to recite passages in the swinging meter characteristic of the island.

page 44 Guillema Conte, who had set up a gym in the city: There is a touching photo of a thin, dreamy, youthful Demitrios, with a bewildered gaze, seated next to the formidably muscled brothers Conte, who are built like a pair of wardrobes. Demitrios's face is narrow, almost feminine, his expression vulnerable.

page 51 "You're just like your mother": Demitrios himself told me this version of how he first heard who his mother was. The same applies to the story of his adventures with Cora.

page 56 he attempted to enlist in the Portuguese army: This is taken from a statement made by Demitrios to the South African police after the murder. I am doubtful of its veracity.

page 58 "Out of control": These are the only words I have put in Demitrios's mouth that I do not know him to have said or written. The picture of his illness given here—in large measure my own reconstruction—is derived both from his later statements and from my knowledge of people in my own circle who, like him, have suffered from similar intermittent periods of profound psychic distress.

page 61 his name resurfaced in the official South African files: A confusion of identities sometimes worked in Demitrios's favor. The officials apparently received no guidance on the transliteration of Greek names; moreover, he had shortened his father's surname. By 1939 there were a number of separate files referring to the same man. The Department of Immigration and Asiatic Affairs had papers on him in File G.8226; the Department of the Interior in Files B.3700 and B.7771.

page 63 the tapering silver leaf of a shrub . . . to the docks: Information given to the writer by Demitrios, March 1998.

page 65 attached to a hospital in Boston: His condition was described by this institution as "psycho-neurosis—mixed type." The six times he was admitted to hospitals between 1943 and 1947—among them the Seamen's Convalescent Home in Oyster Bay, an American army hospital in Great Britain, an institution in Charleston, South Carolina, Ellis Island Hospital in New York, and North Grafton State Hospital in Massachusetts—the diagnoses varied: "schizophrenia"; "subject to a psychosis—type not established"; "constitutional psychopathy and pathologically emotional." Two striking points emerge. First, he fell ill regularly but was as regularly declared healthy and discharged. Second, and more important, he was never hospitalized in southern Africa, which suggests that he was generally in a calmer state of mind when living there.

page 75 The move did nothing to improve his circumstances: Around this time—some weeks after the uprising in Sharpeville—the first, unsuccessful attempt on Verwoerd's life was made. During an agricultural show in Johannesburg, a rich English-speaking farmer, David Pratt, succeeded in shooting the prime minister in the head twice with a small-caliber pistol (a .22, in fact, like the one Demitrios was to buy in Cape Town some seven years later). Verwoerd survived the attack in miraculous fashion: the doctors discovered that the bullets had done little more than clear out his sinuses. In London money was collected for a lawyer to defend Pratt in court, but he committed suicide in a psychiatric hospital in Bloemfontein before the trial could begin.

page 81 A Mr. J. van der Berg, the official responsible: According to reports, van der Berg was extensively investigated and interrogated by the South African security police after the attack on Verwoerd. Subsequently he was discharged from the civil service. He ended up with his family in a shabby district on the outskirts of Durban, a broken man.

page 83 never regarded as a hero: The attitude of the African National Congress is in part responsible. According to the ANC's official account of the incident, the deed was committed by "an obscure *white* messenger" (my italics). The words are those of Nelson Mandela. He follows by saying, "Political assassination is not something that I or the ANC have ever supported" (*Long Walk to Freedom,* London, 1994, p. 417).

For a further indication of the postapartheid government's attitude toward Tsafendas, see my extended note below, pp. 174–75.

page 89 Hanno Probst: Probst recognized an enlarged passport photograph of Demitrios in the *Natal Mercury* fifteen months after their meeting. He made a deposition to the police in Nyoni, stating, "I suspect him of having had an influence over the inhabitants of Mangete. . . . The youth in the reserve became aggressive and obstreperous while he was there. Since the assassination of Dr. Verwoerd order has been re-established and the young men in the area, fortunately, are well under control."

page 112 Manolis, the tall bosun: Manolis Mastromanolis—then thirty-seven years old, today in his early seventies—currently lives in his birthplace, the island of Kos. He refuses to speak of the events described here.

page 116 "We'll get the lot of you!": See *In No Uncertain Terms: Memoirs,* by Helen Suzman (London, 1993), p. 69.

page 116 Verwoerd's lifeless body: The report on the autopsy—which was carried out by Dr. Theodor Gottfried Schwär in the presence of Lieutenant Colonel Buytendag of the South African police—contains an extensive account of the wounds inflicted on Verwoerd. It states also that his brain weighed 1.430 kilograms.

page 118 "The sexual part of it too—the Immorality Act . . .": This comment was withheld from the public, as were Demitrios's seditious remarks in Mozambique about the rainbow flag, which were duly noted by the PIDE. The

Portuguese divulged them on condition that they be kept confidential. The Americans were also reticent in the matter. A coded report marked TOP SECRET was sent from the U.S. embassy in South Africa to the State Department in Washington: "The Department believes that handing over information at this stage could have undesirable consequences . . . since [the] file apparently reveals that Tsafendas is quarter Negro or African."

page 134 Evolution of the Species: Obviously Demitrios meant *Origin of the Species*.

page 141 Why was he still confined in the wretched institution . . . ?: Within a few days of my last meeting with Demitrios I wrote a letter to Archbishop Desmond Tutu, then the chairman of the Truth and Reconciliation Commission (TRC), asking for some form of amnesty and reparation to be granted to him. This plea did not seem unreasonable, for Demitrios's motives at the time of the assassination had been political as well as personal; he had identified strongly with the country's colored and black populations and felt himself to have been part of a wider movement of protest. My hope in making this representation was that he might be allowed to spend whatever days remained to him in the relative comfort of a private clinic. I was ignorant of the fact that several months previously a similar submission to the TRC had been made by Liza Key, the filmmaker mentioned in the Epilogue.

During the latter half of 1998 Demitrios was moved to a

more comfortable section of Sterkfontein Hospital. I do not know whether this was a consequence of the approaches made by Ms. Key and me. What is certain is that, after a formal acknowledgment, my letter was passed on to the Ministry of Health, which procrastinated for a full five months before replying to it. On the eve of the publication of my book in Dutch, I finally heard from the minister herself, Dr. Dlamini Zuma. She thanked me for the interest I had shown "in Mr. Tsafendas's health conditions [*sic*]" and assured me that she was confident that he was receiving the care and attention he needed. "As his personal safety is also of concern," her letter continued, "we believe that his present environment is conducive" (conducive to what? I wondered). She went on to explain that "a private facility could not offer the secure environment required as threats to his life are still a possibility." And to forestall any further questions I was told flatly that "the State does not pay for patients in private institutions."

So there the matter remained. And there he remained, to the end.

page 150 the dilemma of the "baster": I am indebted here to insights brilliantly expressed by V. A. February in *Mind Your Colour: The 'Coloured' Stereotype in South African Literature* (London, 1981).

page 159 the eighty-one-year-old patient finally succumbed: According to a reliable source, Demitrios had insisted on making a will or testament of some sort several years earlier.

In it he is said to have stipulated that his body undergo an autopsy, so that his "worm" might be exposed to the eye of science at last. I have been unable to find out whether his wishes were heeded.

I owe many thanks to the staff of the South African National Library and the Parliamentary Library, both in Cape Town, and of the State Archives in Pretoria, who served me tirelessly. A word of gratitude is due to the doctors and staff of the hospital in Sterkfontein and to the countless South Africans who assisted me over the years with advice, action, and a listening ear and who supported me with generous offers of hospitality. I can name only a few of them here: Ernest Lindenberg and Hazel Moolman, Peter and Barbara Knox-Shaw, Antjie Krog, Derick Eaves, Ampie Coetzee, Breyten Breytenbach.

For the guiding artistic concept by which I have worked, I owe special thanks to my dear, living muse, Nicole Müller, without whose insight, patience, and sense of humor this book would never have appeared in print.

ABOUT THE AUTHOR

HENK VAN WOERDEN, a prizewinning author, was born in the
Netherlands in 1947. He moved to South Africa as a child,
studied art at the University of Cape Town, and in 1968
returned to Amsterdam, where he lives today. *The Assassin* has
been nominated for two major Dutch awards and translated
into five languages.

ABOUT THE TRANSLATOR

DAN JACOBSON grew up in Kimberley, South Africa, and has
been living in England for many years. The author of novels,
short stories, travel books, and essays, his most recent book is
Heshel's Kingdom, a family memoir.